STARTUP SMART

THE GIRLS' GUIDE TO ENTREPRENEURSHIP

Alison Hall, CPA

First paperback edition August 2023

Book design by Ljiljana Pavkov / bookwormsdesign.com

ISBN 979-8-9887897-0-3

Published by The Boldest ME LLC
www.theboldestmekids.com

TABLE OF CONTENTS

FORWARD   7

INTRODUCTION   11

Chapter 1:
    ↳UNLEASHING YOUR INNER ENTREPRENEUR   13

Chapter 2:
    ↳IT STARTS WITH AN IDEA: USING YOUR IMAGINATION   23

Chapter 3:
    ↳THE POWER OF MENTORSHIP: LEARNING FROM THE BEST   37

Chapter 4:
    ↳BUSINESS BASICS: UNDERSTANDING MONEY MATTERS   45

Chapter 5:
    ↳YOUR BUSINESS PLAN - ROADMAP TO SUCCESS   53

Chapter 6:
    ↳HOW TO GET MONEY TO START YOUR BUSINESS OR KEEP IT RUNNING 59

Chapter 7:
    ↳PRICING AND COSTS   67

Chapter 8:
    ↳THE LEGAL STUFF AND TAXES MADE SIMPLE   75

Chapter 9:
    ↳MARKETING: HOW TO LET PEOPLE KNOW ABOUT YOUR
     AWESOME PRODUCT OR SERVICE   79

Chapter 10:
    ↳BUILDING YOUR STRENGTHS: THE ENTREPRENEURIAL TOOLKIT   91

Chapter 11:
    ↳SECURING YOUR FINANCIAL FUTURE   97

Chapter 12:
    ↳LOOKING AHEAD: THE FUTURE IS YOURS!   103

Chapter 13:
    ↳PARENTS' GUIDE TO NURTURING ENTREPRENEURIAL MINDS   111

STARTUP SMART

THE GIRLS' GUIDE TO ENTREPRENEURSHIP

FORWARD

TO THE PARENTS, GUARDIANS, MENTORS, AND ARDENT SUPPORTERS WHO BOUGHT THIS BOOK FOR A CHILD,

I am thrilled to share with you my passion for starting and running businesses, and the incredible opportunities it can bring. When I was a kid, my first business was the classic lemonade stand. I dragged a folding table down our long, gravel driveway, painted a cardboard sign with 'Lemonade Sold Here' on it, and propped it up against the mailbox. As the ice melted, I sat for what seemed like hours waiting for my first customer. I still remember the waxy feel of the little paper cups I fiddled with and eventually poured lukewarm lemonade into. We lived on a dead-end road with maybe 20 houses in a small town in Connecticut. Not exactly a traffic hub. Eventually neighbors began to trickle through, though, and like any good neighbors, they stopped each time they passed by.

I had what I thought was a good run for a day or two, and I was fully prepared to hunker down for the summer. My mother, however, suggested that I move on to other pursuits. While both of my parents were white collar professionals with no entrepreneurial expertise, the importance of location and a willing target market weren't lost on them. She knew that our neighbors were being kind and that my lemonade days were numbered.

My next entrepreneurial enterprise did capitalize on location, as well as meeting customer demand, and cornering the market. I sold candy at my school. Not just any candy, mind you. Candy from around the world. My dad traveled extensively for work and would bring me bags of treats from whatever region he had visited. While I enjoyed candy as much as the next kid, I saw an opportunity to provide a hot commodity to my fellow students and make a buck while I was at it. Since the candy kept changing, my customers were always curious about the latest batch.

My other youthful forays into entrepreneurship were straightforward: baby and pet sitting, tutoring, and teaching swimming and sailing. At the time I didn't even know what an entrepreneur was, and I certainly didn't consider myself to be a business owner. I was just a kid trying out different things and earning a little money along the way.

While there is no precise global statistic regarding the number of kids who have started businesses, there has been a growing trend in recent years. Young people have more access than ever before to information, technological advancements, and entrepreneurial education and support programs, but we cannot do enough to create environments where kids, and girls in particular, can be inspired and empowered to start their own businesses at an early age.

I wrote this book because I would have loved to have one like it when I was young. In fact, I originally wrote a similar book for women I work with in my coaching practice. I wanted to be able to offer them a succinct, practical overview of how to start a business, with enough detail to be useful and informative, but not so much as to be overwhelming. I found myself thinking about how many women's lives might have been different if they had been introduced to entrepreneurship early on. So, while there is nothing on these pages, or in the more advanced companion edition, that does not apply to all young aspiring business owners, I did write this with young girls in mind.

Encouraging and supporting the entrepreneurial spirit in young people is vital as it can foster valuable skills, creativity, and a strong work ethic. Girls have unlimited potential to innovate and shape the world around them and I want to help equip them with the tools, mindset, and confidence to turn their ideas into reality. Whether it's a lemonade stand, an online shop, or a tech startup, starting a small business can provide valuable learning experiences and lay the foundation for a wide array of future endeavors.

Some readers will learn everything they need to know about how to launch their first business from this book. For those who want to take their businesses to the next level by growing or diversifying, or truly making it a profitable ongoing business, the subsequent book in this series explores more advanced topics relevant to entrepreneurs of all ages. While the young business owners highlighted in each chapter are fictional, they are based on real girls running real businesses around the globe.

There are many additional topics your child may want to explore, and activities to help them solidify the concepts, that can be found on our website **http://TheBoldestMeKids.com**. Your child will not only find information to feed their entrepreneurial curiosity, but content that speaks to them holistically.

They will find:

↳ 50+ business ideas for kids

↳ More sample business plans

↳ Glossary of Financial and Entrepreneurial Terms and Concepts

↳ Entrepreneur's Troubleshooting Guide

- ↳ Programs, Camps and Courses
- ↳ Scholarships
- ↳ Recommended Books
- ↳ How to Sell Successfully
- ↳ Negotiate Like a Pro
- ↳ Provide Great Customer Service
- ↳ Accounting and Recordkeeping
- ↳ Creating a Crowdfunding Campaign
- ↳ Strengths and Values Quizzes
- ↳ Resources to Help You Be the Best You

The **Startup Smart – The Girls' Guide to Entrepreneurship Workbook** is an additional resource to help your child get the most out of this book. It includes the activities found in the book as well as bonus activities designed to enhance learning.

The future of entrepreneurship is bright, and girls and women will play a crucial role in shaping it. We need innovative thinkers, problem solvers, and trailblazers to bring fresh ideas to the table, and I hope this book can help give the next generation a head start!

Alison Hall,
CPA and Serial Entrepreneur

P.S.: *Thank you, Elle, for encouraging me to write about a subject I'm passionate about for an audience that's going to run this world. I'm so incredibly grateful to have you as my partner in life, business, and grand thoughts.*

INTRODUCTION

WELCOME TO THE EXCITING WORLD OF ENTREPRENEURSHIP! THIS IS A PLACE TO USE YOUR IMAGINATION, BE CREATIVE, AND THINK ABOUT BIG IDEAS FOR YOUR FUTURE.

But what is entrepreneurship? Well, it's a long word to describe using your unique talents, skills, and ideas to create something extraordinary and make a positive impact on the world around you.

Entrepreneurs are very important to the world because they are the ones who come up with new ideas, inventions, and technologies, and they create businesses. They use their imaginations to create new products and services that make our lives easier, more convenient, more fun, and make the world a better place. They are the engines that drive progress and help society move forward.

Entrepreneurs take risks and work hard to bring their ideas to life. They create jobs for people, which helps the economy and allows employees to support their families. When entrepreneurs succeed, they often give back to their communities by donating to charities or starting programs to help others.

Think about some things you use every day, like your tablet or your dog's favorite toy. Someone had to come up with the idea and start a company to make those things. That person was an entrepreneur. They saw a need or an opportunity and made it happen.

Entrepreneurship teaches us that anything is possible. It shows us that no dream is too big or too small, and that every idea has the potential to blossom into something incredible. It's all about embracing what's important – your passion, curiosity, and ability to bounce back from setbacks.

Throughout this book you'll learn how to transform your ideas into thriving businesses. We'll explore the importance of evaluating your ideas, problem-solving, and following through. We'll discuss how to turn challenges into opportunities, and how each challenge can make you stronger and more determined to succeed.

You will learn how to create a business plan, how to market your product or service, how to keep track of your money, and many other valuable lessons.

The stories of young entrepreneurs, the practical advice, fun activities, and exercises will help you develop the skills you will need to run your business properly.

The most successful entrepreneurs do their best work, and have the most fun, when they're supported by others and working in teams, so bring your family and friends into the activities!

It is never too early to start pursuing your entrepreneurial dreams. Whether it's creating games on Roblox, dog walking, or designing and selling cool t-shirts, every move you make today can be a steppingstone to a future filled with possibilities.

So, are you ready to get started? Let's dive in and remember, the world is waiting for your unique ideas, talents, and perspective. Believe in yourself, dream big, and let your entrepreneurial spirit soar!

Chapter 1:

UNLEASHING YOUR INNER ENTREPRENEUR

You have brains in your head.
You have feet in your shoes.
You can steer yourself in any
direction you choose.

DR. SEUSS
Oh the Places You'll Go!

↳ Do you dream of creating something amazing that will change the world?

↳ Are you itching to start a small business doing something you absolutely love?

IF YoU ANSWERED YES To EITHER oF THESE QUESTIoNS, YoU'RE ALREADY SHoWING SIGNS oF BECoMING AN ENTREPRENEUR!

But what is an entrepreneur, exactly? An entrepreneur is a person who comes up with creative ideas and takes risks to start their own business. They use their imagination and hard work to turn their ideas into something real. Entrepreneurs are problem solvers who see opportunities and find ways to make them happen. They are enthusiastic, determined, and willing to learn from both their successes and mistakes. As an entrepreneur, you get to be the boss of your own business and have the freedom to make decisions and create something special. It can be anything from starting a lemonade stand in your neighborhood to designing and selling painted rocks online. Entrepreneurs can turn any idea into a reality.

Imagine this: You've noticed that your friends and family are always losing their sunglasses. "Hmm," you think, "What if there were sunglasses with a built-in tracker, so they could never get lost?" So, you design this tracker, assemble a few pairs of prototype (a fancy word for your first version)

sunglasses with the tracker attached and then you start selling them. Voila! You've just become an entrepreneur.

Don't worry if you think your idea might be too simple or too 'out there'. Some of the best businesses started with the simplest of ideas. Google started as an idea for a better search engine, and now it's a huge company that does so much more.

As an entrepreneur, you'll learn so many fantastic skills. You'll learn how to plan, manage money, sell, and most importantly, solve problems. In this book, you'll explore what it takes to be an entrepreneur, and discover the skills you'll need to be successful. Along the way you will read the stories of other young entrepreneurs.

WHAT DoES IT TAKE To BE AN ENTREPRENEUR?

Now that we've learned what an entrepreneur is, let's dive into what it takes to become one. You might be thinking, "Do I need to be super smart or have a lot of money to start?" The answer is "no." The most successful entrepreneurs are those who are curious and aren't afraid to make mistakes.

So, let's break down exactly what it takes to become an entrepreneur:

- **Passion:** What are the things that you absolutely love to do? Maybe you enjoy baking cupcakes, or you're always the first one to create a new dance routine for your friends. Your passion is the thing that gets you excited and makes you feel alive. When you build a business around something you're excited about, it's like adding fuel to your entrepreneurial engine.

- **Curiosity:** This is your superpower for coming up with new ideas. Ask questions about everything! Why do people like certain things? How can something work better? What if we try it a different way? Remember the sunglass tracker idea? That started from asking the simple question: "What if there was a pair of sunglasses that couldn't get lost?"

- **Courage:** Not the 'fight a dragon' kind of courage, but the courage to take risks and face the unknown. Being an entrepreneur means stepping out of your comfort zone and trying new things. You might make mistakes, and that's totally okay! In fact, mistakes can be your best teachers.

- **Perseverance:** This just means that you never give up, even when things get tough. There might be times when your idea doesn't work out the way you want it to, or when others don't believe in it. This is where perseverance comes in. It's about pushing through the challenges and bouncing back from failures. Remember, every great entrepreneur faces obstacles, and learning to overcome obstacles is what helps us become stronger. The stronger we become, the better able we are to overcome obstacles and that's called 'resilience.'

- **Creativity:** Lastly, you need a dash of creativity. This isn't just about being able to draw or design, but about thinking differently and coming up with innovative or unique solutions to problems.

And the best thing about all these traits? You already have them! As a human being, you already have the ability to be passionate, curious, brave, persistent, and creative. So yes, you have what it takes to be a successful entrepreneur. You may just need to sharpen your skills and the best way to do that is by practicing in real life.

PRODUCTS VERSUS SERVICES: WHAT DO YOU NEED TO KNOW?

Now that we know what it takes to be an entrepreneur, let's dive into something equally exciting - understanding what you can offer as an entrepreneur. There are two main things that businesses provide: products and services. But what's the difference between them, and how do you choose what to offer?

→ **Products:** These are physical things that you can make, sell, and people can use. Think about a scrumptious cake from a bakery, a beautifully crafted bracelet, or a fun board game - these are all products. Products can be great if you enjoy making things with your hands, or if you have a fantastic idea for something new that people would love. An important thing to remember about products is that they need to be made which means someone (labor) or something (machine) has to make them; you need to buy supplies; the products need to be stored somewhere until they're sold; and they need to be delivered to the customer.

Let's say you love painting, and you decide to create colorful, painted tote bags. Your product is the tote bag, but the magic you add is your special, hand-painted design. Each tote bag you paint is a product that you can sell.

→ **Services:** Unlike products, services aren't things that you can touch or hold. Services are things you do to help others. For example, a dog-walking service, a dance class, or even helping people organize their birthday parties - these are all services. If you enjoy helping others and are good at doing something that people need, offering a service could be perfect for you. With services, instead of making a physical item, you're spending your time making someone's life easier or more enjoyable.

Imagine that you're good at playing the guitar and you love music. You could start a service teaching other kids how to play the guitar. Each lesson you give is a service you provide.

So, how do you decide between a product and a service? Well, it depends on what you love doing and where your talents shine. The best part about being an entrepreneur is that you get to choose what your business is all about. So, what excites you most - making things or helping others?

Let's meet some young entrepreneurs who started their journeys early and learned from their first ventures. We'll explore Chloe's jewelry business, Nia's tutoring services, and Julien's classic lemonade stand.

CHLOE'S CRYSTALS:
SPARKLING SUCCESS IN THE WORLD OF HANDMADE JEWELRY

When Chloe was 10 years old, she stumbled upon a hidden gem that would shape her future—her love for shiny, beautiful crystals. She loved their unique colors and patterns, and she was captivated by their beauty.

Driven by her passion for crystals and a desire to share their beauty with the world, Chloe decided to turn her hobby into a business. She read books and watched YouTube videos to learn about the different types of crystals, and how to turn them into wearable art.

Chloe worked hard to perfect her techniques and to create stunning pieces of crystal jewelry. She asked for feedback from friends and family, carefully listening to their opinions and suggestions.

As Chloe's skills and confidence grew, she decided to sell her jewelry at local craft fairs. After setting up her decorated booth, she was delighted when people began to buy her jewelry. Word quickly spread about Chloe's unique handmade jewelry, and she sold more than she had expected.

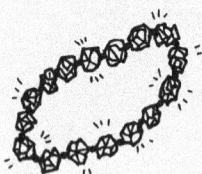

Next Chloe built a website to show off her creations, using photos and fun descriptions. Through social media platforms that her parents authorized, she shared her journey, interacted with customers, and showed her latest designs. Her online store allowed her to connect with customers from all over the world, spreading the joy and beauty of crystals.

Chloe's excellent customer service her a loyal following of crystal enthusiasts who eagerly awaited her designs.

Her business did so well that Chloe decided to donate a portion of her profits to organizations that supported environmental causes and crystal conservation efforts. By combining her love for crystals with a desire to make a positive impact, Chloe became not only an entrepreneur but also an environmentalist, helping the world in her small way.

NIA'S TUTORING TRIUMPH, ONE LESSON AT A TIME

At the age of 11 Nia, an avid reader, discovered that she had a talent for helping her schoolmates understand tough course work, so she decided to use her skills to launch a tutoring business – Nia's Tutoring Triumph.

Starting small, she initially offered her tutoring services to her classmates who struggled with subjects that she was good at like English and math. As word spread, Nia's reputation as an exceptional tutor grew and she realized that she could also help younger students in her school, providing them with the same patient support she offered her classmates.

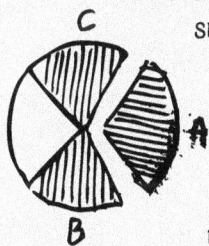

As Nia's tutoring sessions progressed, the results spoke for themselves. Students who once struggled to understand certain subjects were getting much better grades, and they were building confidence. Nia's tutoring sessions became a safe space where students felt comfortable asking questions, exploring new ideas, and learning.

Nia knew that, even though her tutoring business was a success, it was important to keep up with her own schoolwork and after school activities, so she managed her time carefully. She made a schedule that included time for all the important things in her life like homework, chores, spending time with her family, hobbies and sports, as well as tutoring. This balance helped her to feel in control, successful and strong.

JULIEN'S LEMONADE STAND,
CLASSIC FIRST VENTURE

At 10 years old Julien and her family moved Las Vegas, Nevada, known for its scorching hot summer temperatures. To beat the heat, Julien's mom made a habit of whipping up delicious batches of homemade lemonade that Julien and her new friends would gulp down throughout the long summer days.

One sweltering afternoon Julien came up with an idea, "Maybe the neighbors would love Mom's delicious lemonade too!" With her mother's enthusiastic support, Julien set out to bring her lemonade to the hot and thirsty community by setting up her very own lemonade stand in the front yard.

She started by following her mom's lemonade recipe and filling several pitchers with her new product. Then, with a folding table, red plastic cups, ice and colorful handmade signs, Julien's Lemonade Stand was born. To her delight, residents were quick to stop by to try her homemade thirst quencher, and word of mouth brought new customers each day.

As she managed her stand, Julien not only learned how to count out the correct change to give customers when they paid with cash, and how to keep track of her earnings, but she also discovered the concept of 'supply and demand'. On really hot days, when more people wanted to buy her refreshing lemonade, she had to plan ahead and prepare larger batches. She worked on her customer service skills, giving each customer a warm smile and thanking them for their purchase.

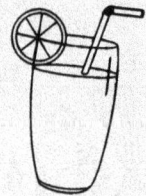

Julien learned that she had the power to earn money while bringing joy to others and helping her community.

Keep these girls' stories in mind as you think about what you might do for your own entrepreneurial venture!

SUGGESTED ACTIVITY: CREATE YOUR VISION BOARD

A vision board is a collage that you put your dreams on so that when you look at it, it's easy to focus on what you want in your life and be inspired to believe in yourself.

You can make a vision board in different ways. Some people cut pictures out of magazines or print them from the internet and stick them onto poster boards. Others create a digital vision board using templates or apps.

You're going to make your own vision board using supplies you probably have around the house.

MATERIALS NEEDED

1. A large piece of cardboard or poster board.
2. Old magazines, newspapers, or printed images.
3. Glue or tape.
4. Scissors.
5. Markers or colored pencils.
6. Stickers, glitter, or any other decorative craft supplies you have (optional).

INSTRUCTIONS

Dream Big: Start by thinking about what you'd love to achieve in your life....or before you reach a certain age. It might be starting your own business, inventing a new product, helping your community, or even changing the world! Anything goes, so don't hold back.

If the thought of starting a business excites you, you don't need to know what kind of business yet or whether it's possible. Just focus on the big picture and create a board that represents your vision.

Gather Your Materials: Look through your magazines, newspapers, or printed images and cut out pictures and words that match up with your dreams and goals. They can be related to the business you want to create or things you want to accomplish or places you want to go.

↳ **Arrange Your Vision and Glue it Down:** Before you start gluing, arrange your pictures and words on your board so that it creates a story. Remember, there's no right or wrong way to do this. It's all about what inspires you. Once you're happy with your layout, glue, or tape everything down. Feel free to add decorations.

↳ **Display Your Vision Board:** Find a place to hang your vision board where you'll see it every day. This will be a constant reminder of your goals and what you're working towards.

As you continue to learn and grow, you might find that your goals change, and that's okay. Feel free to update your vision board whenever you feel like it. Remember, being an entrepreneur is all about being adaptable and open to change.

Chapter 2:

IT STARTS WITH AN IDEA: USING YOUR IMAGINATION

Dream big.
Start small.
But most of all, start.

MARISSA MAYER
Former CEO of Yahoo

WHAT'S YOUR BIG IDEA?

Ever heard of the phrase, "it all starts with an idea"? Well, it's true, especially in the world of entrepreneurship. Whether it's a new gadget to make life easier, a fun game that brings people joy, or a service that meets a need in your community, every business starts as a single spark of an idea.

You may be thinking, "But how do I come up with a 'big idea'?" The first thing you need to know is that ideas don't just pop into our heads fully formed and ready to go. They usually start as tiny thoughts or observations that we think about over time.

You know when you're daydreaming and suddenly a great idea comes to you? Or maybe when you're doing chores and you think, "There must be a better way to do this"? Those moments are where big ideas start.

But ideas aren't worth much if they stay locked in your head. They need to be shared, tested, and shaped into reality. So, let's figure out how to catch those idea sparks and turn them into roaring idea fires.

IDENTIFYING YOUR INTERESTS

Start by thinking about what you're enthusiastic about. Do you love animals, art, sports, or solving puzzles? Maybe you love helping others or making a difference in your community.

Your interests are a great place to start when you're looking for a big idea. If you pick something that you care about, it will be a lot easier to stay motivated to do what it takes to grow the idea.

SPOTTING PROBLEMS TO SOLVE

Keep your eyes and ears open for problems that need solving. These could be things that frustrate you, challenges you see other people face, or issues in your community. The best ideas often come from someone saying, "This could be better, and I think I know how."

IMAGINATION AND CREATIVITY

Allow yourself to dream and be creative. What if you could invent something new? What would it be? How would it work? Think about the things that you're good at and the things you've enjoyed doing. When it comes to ideas, it helps if it's something that interests you or something you'd like to learn more about. There's no limit to what you can imagine!

SO, WHAT'S YOUR BIG IDEA?

Don't worry if you don't have it figured out yet. For now, stay curious and be open to the endless possibilities around you.

HoW To NURTURE AND DEVELoP YoUR IDEAS

So, you think you've come up with a brilliant idea. Now what? Do you just rush off and start selling it? Not quite. Just like a tiny seed needs sunlight, water, and care to grow into a big strong tree, your idea needs care and feeding too.

RESEARCH, RESEARCH, RESEARCH

The first step to nurturing your idea is research. Why research? Well, to make sure your idea is special enough so that people would want or need it. You can do this by searching the internet, reading books or magazines, and even talking to people to gather information.

Ask yourself questions like:

↳ Is there already a product or service like my idea?

↳ Is anyone in my area providing this product or service?

↳ How can I make my idea better or different?

↳ Who would want or need my product or service?

↳ How could it help them?

↳ Would people be willing to pay for my service or product? *

> *** This is VERY important. If there's no market for your product or service (meaning, no one is willing to pay you for it), your idea is a hobby, not a business. That's fine, but it's important to know the difference.**

Your research will help you understand your idea better and figure out ways to make it shine.

BRAINSToRMING

Once you've done your research, it's time to let your creativity flow again. Sketch out your idea or write down notes to describe it. As you brainstorm, you will come up with new ways to look at your idea that you hadn't thought of before. Take your time with this step and look at all the angles.

GETTING FEEDBACK

Feedback is important so don't be afraid to share your ideas with others and ask for their opinions. This could be your family, friends, or teachers. They might be able to give you suggestions that you hadn't thought of.

Not all feedback will be positive, and that's okay. Don't let negative feedback get you down. Instead, look at it as an opportunity to improve your idea, and always be sure to thank anyone who took the time to give you honest feedback.

ITERATE AND IMPROVE

Based on the feedback you receive and your own thoughts, you may need to make changes to your idea. This process is called 'iteration' and it's an important part of developing your idea into something that really works. You may go through several iterations as you continue to work toward a product or service idea that people will want to pay for.

DOCUMENT YOUR PROGRESS

Keep a journal or digital document of your research findings, sketches, feedback, and changes. Not only will this help you keep track of your progress, but it will also be a fun way to look back and see how your idea has grown over time.

TEST YOUR BIG IDEA

OK, so you've come up with a fantastic idea you feel good about. Before you dash off to make your first million, it's time to put your big idea to the test. This stage is important because you'll find out if your product or service really does have what it takes to succeed.

Testing is just trying out your idea in real life to see how it works and if people are interested. One of the biggest mistakes you can make as an entrepreneur is to move ahead without testing.

For example, if you're planning to sell custom-designed t-shirts, you create a single t-shirt with your design and use that t-shirt as a test to see if people would want to buy it. That one test t-shirt is your prototype. If your idea is a pet sitting service, your prototype could be a flyer explaining what you offer. Once you have your prototype ready, think about how much you want to charge for your product or service. We'll discuss pricing in a later chapter, but for right now you would pick a price you think makes sense and let your testers give you feedback.

GATHER A TEST GROUP, RUN YOUR TEST AND COLLECT FEEDBACK

A test group is a small group of people who try out your prototype. They could be your family, friends, neighbors, or classmates. Make sure you choose people who will understand your product or service, and who will give you helpful comments.

Let your test group try out your prototype. Encourage them to be honest. What did they like? What didn't they like? What would they change? Pay attention to their reactions and be open to their suggestions. Do they seem interested and excited, or do they look confused and unimproccod? Romombor, your goal is to make your product or service as amazing as possible, so do your best to keep your feelings out of it. Helpful feedback can feel hurtful sometimes, but as an entrepreneur it's very important to be able to accept suggestions.

ANALYZE AND ADJUST

Use the feedback from your test group to make changes and improvements to your idea. This might mean tweaking your design or adjusting your prices, or making some other change based on the feedback.

Maybe your homemade soap will sell better at a local craft fair than online. Or maybe your pet sitting service needs to offer something extra, like pet grooming, to stand out from the competition. The key is to keep learning and trying.

WHAT TO DO IF YOUR BIG IDEA IS A FLOP

Let's imagine for a moment that you've come up with a fantastic idea. But instead of the roaring applause you expected, you're met with…meh. Your idea, it turns out, is not a winner. What do you do?

Well, don't let this burst your bubble! Not every idea is going to be a hit, and that's perfectly okay. Most entrepreneurs face setbacks and many must start at the beginning with a brand-new idea.

Even though it might feel like the end of the world, remember that every setback is a chance to learn something new. The most successful entrepreneurs are the ones who don't let failure get them down but use it as a chance to grow and improve.

WHAT WENT WRONG?

Take a close look at your idea. Did it fail because it wasn't interesting or useful?

Was it too expensive? Or was there another reason? Understanding what went wrong can help you avoid the same mistakes in the future. Listen to what your test group liked and disliked about your idea and come up with a better idea next time.

LILY'S HEALTHY SNACKS:
A FLAVORFUL SUCCESS

By the time she was 11 years old, Lily had two things she was incredibly passionate about: her love for food and her concern about health. Her family had a history of diabetes, and she worried about their unhealthy eating habits, especially when it came to snacking.

Lily was frustrated by the fact that snacks available at her local food stores were either boring or not healthy. Sugar-packed cookies, chips with lots of salt, and artificial fruit juices made up the options. Lily's lightbulb moment can when she thought, "Why not make my own snacks that are both delicious and healthy?"

She started experimenting with recipes at home, testing combinations of nuts, dried fruits, oats, honey, and dark chocolate to create the perfect healthy snack bar. Lily's family and friends became her taste testers. After lots of attempts, and some epic failures, Lily finally came up with a recipe that was a hit with everyone.

Next, she decided to test her big idea more widely. She baked a big batch of her healthy snack bars and set up a table in her school hallway during lunch period, and at her brother's soccer matches. The response was beyond her wildest dreams. People loved the taste and the idea of having a healthy snack option. Kids at school bought out her entire stock, and parents placed orders to buy for their families.

Encouraged by this success, Lily started 'Lily's Healthy Snacks.' She continued to sell at school and soccer and added the farmers' market along with taking orders over the phone. Lily had identified a problem and a creative solution.

Even when her first few recipes didn't work out as she had hoped, Lily didn't give up. Instead, she accepted feedback and continued to improve her recipe until she created a product that met her needs and goals. Creativity and being unwilling to give up, also known as 'perseverance', can turn a little idea into a tasty success.

MIA'S MARVELOUS
SOAPS SOLUTION

At just 10 years old, Mia noticed a problem that lots of people face: her younger sister had sensitive skin that was constantly irritated by harsh chemicals found in body washes and soaps found in regular stores. Seeing how itchy and uncomfortable her sister was, Mia was determined to find a solution.

She dove into research on natural ingredients and their benefits for sensitive skin. With her mom's help, she spent hours experimenting with different combinations of herbs and essential oils to create a gentle and effective formula. After months of trial and error, Mia finally developed a handmade, chemical-free soap that worked perfectly for her sister's sensitive skin.

Mia was excited about her creation and wanted to share it with other people who had skin issues like her sister's. She started by giving samples of her soap to her family and

friends. People loved it so she decided to turn her passion into a business and named it" Mia's Marvelous Soaps".

She set up a small workshop in her parent's basement and, with their help, she bought ingredients and made batches of her handmade soaps that she sold online and at craft fairs. Her 18-year-old brother helped her create and manage social media accounts where she posted pictures of her products and the ingredients she used, and videos of herself making the soap.

Mia expanded her product line to include a variety of skincare products like lotions and lip balms, all made with natural and eco-friendly ingredients, and she carefully packaged her creations in biodegradable materials.

What began as a solution for her sister's skin sensitivity turned into a thriving business for Mia.

ALEX
CONTROLS THE CONTROLLER

Alex, a 12-year-old with a love for video games, noticed a common frustration among gamers—confusing controls. Determined to find a solution, she put her creative mind to work. She started by sketching a design for a video game controller that would make gameplay smoother and more enjoyable.

Excited about her idea, Alex shared her design with her parents, who recognized her talent and supported her vision. With the help of a 3D printer, they turned Alex's design into a real-life prototype of the controller she had imagined. Alex was thrilled to hold it in her hands.

She reached out to fellow gamers where she put together gaming sessions to introduce her new controller, and the response was nothing but positive! They loved the user-friendly design and the improved gameplay experience it offered. Word quickly spread about Alex's invention, and her peers began asking where they could get their hands on one.

Inspired by the positive feedback, Alex and her parents decided to turn her idea into a real business. They launched an online campaign to raise money from people who believed in Alex's invention and were willing to pledge money to help her launch her business and make lots of controllers for gamers to use worldwide.

The campaign was a huge success, Alex received enough money to make the new controllers, and her story received attention from major tech magazines and online platforms. With the funds raised, Alex and her parents partnered with a manufacturer to produce the controllers on a larger scale.

Alex's video game controllers eventually sold worldwide and she continued to refine her products, listening to feedback from gamers and incorporating their suggestions into new versions. Alex not only made an impact on the gaming industry but also inspired other young inventors to pursue their ideas and make a difference in the world of technology.

Alex's story serves as an example of how a young entrepreneur's creativity, determination, and passion can lead to the development of groundbreaking inventions. By identifying a problem, using her skills to create a solution, and harnessing the power of crowdfunding, Alex proved that age is no barrier to success.

Lily, Mia, and Alex each started with a problem in their everyday lives. By thinking creatively and believing in their ideas, they turned these problems into successful businesses. Innovation often starts with a simple question: "How can I fix this?" or "How can I make this better?"

SUGGESTED ACTIVITY: BRAINSTORMING AND IDEA JOURNALING

This activity will help you tap into your creativity and maybe even discover your very own big idea.

MATERIALS NEEDED:

- A notebook or journal
- A pen or pencil
- Stickers, colored pens, or pencils for decoration (optional)

INSTRUCTIONS

↪ **1. Set aside quiet time:** Find a peaceful spot where you can think without distractions. This could be your bedroom, a corner of your living room, the library, or a spot outside.

↪ **2. Let your mind wander:** Close your eyes and imagine yourself in a world where anything is possible. There are no wrong ideas in brainstorming, so let your imagination run wild. Think about problems you, your friends, or your family experience, as well as the dreams that you have for your future.

↪ **3. Capture your thoughts**: Open your eyes and start writing down all your thoughts, no matter how crazy they may seem. Write down every idea that comes to your mind, even if you think it's too simple, too hard, or too silly. Remember, lots of great businesses started from "silly" ideas.

↪ **4. Brainstorm solutions**: Once you've written down every problem you're interested in solving, brainstorm potential solutions. One of these solutions just might end up being your big idea.

↪ **5. Make it a habit:** Try to spend a few minutes each day jotting down new ideas, observations, and inspirations. As days go by, you'll find that it gets easier and even more fun.

6. Review and Reflect: After a week, look back on what you've written. Are there any patterns? Any ideas that really excite you? Pick out a few favorites and think about how they could be turned into a real-life product or service.

The purpose of this activity is not to come up with a perfect business idea right away. It's about learning to tap into your creativity, identify problems, and think of creative solutions. Have fun, and who knows? Your next big idea could be just a brainstorming session away.

SUGGESTED ACTIVITY: IDEA VALIDATION EXPERIMENT

Now that you have some exciting ideas in your journal, it's time to test them out. This process is called "idea validation," and it's all about figuring out if your idea has the potential to turn into a successful business.

MATERIALS NEEDED:

- Your Idea Journal from the previous activity
- A pen or pencil
- Internet access for research (optional)

INSTRUCTIONS

Here's how to do your own idea validation experiment:

1. **Choose Your Idea:** Look at the ideas in your journal and pick the one that excites you the most.

2. **Define the Problem**: Write down the problem your idea is solving. Is it a big enough problem that people would pay for a solution?

3. **Identify Your Target Audience:** Think about who has this problem. Is it kids your age? Parents? Teachers? Pet owners? The more specific you can be, the better.

4. **Get Feedback:** Talk to people who are part of your target audience. Do they think your solution could solve their problem? Would they be interested in it?

> **Be careful about sharing your ideas with people you don't know well. It's best to discuss with a parent, guardian, or family member first.**

5. **Research the Competition:** Look up similar products or services online. How is your idea different or better?

6. **Tweak Your Idea:** Based on the feedback and research, adjust your idea. Maybe you'll find a better way to solve the problem, or maybe you'll discover a different problem that needs solving.

7. **Record:** Write down everything you've learned in your Idea Journal. It's always fun to look back to see where you came from.

If your idea doesn't pass the validation test, that's okay. Most successful entrepreneurs have had to go back to the drawing board more than once. The important thing is not to be afraid to try again.

SUGGESTED ACTIVITY: DON'T TAKE IT PERSONALLY AND CARRY ON

When your ideas don't work out the way you'd hoped, remember that every "no" or "fail" is a steppingstone to a "yes" and a success. For this activity, let's focus on handling disappointment.

MATERIALS NEEDED:
- Your Idea Journal
- A pen or pencil
- Comfortable space to sit and think

INSTRUCTIONS

↳ **1. Think:** Think about when things didn't go as planned with an idea. It can be an idea you just worked on in the last two activities, or something else in your life. Write about it in your Idea Journal.

↳ **2. Analyze:** What exactly happened? Why do you think things didn't go the way you planned? What did you learn from it? Write the answers in your Idea Journal.

↳ **3. Write a Positive Affirmation:** Think of a positive statement that can help you remember not to take failures personally and to keep going. For example, you could write, "Each failure is a lesson that gets me closer to success," or "I am brave and will keep trying until I succeed." It doesn't matter what you select as long as it's motivational to you.

↳ **4. Carry On:** Write down three things you can do the next time things don't go as planned. Maybe you can talk to a supportive friend, or take a break and do something fun, or start over with a fresh idea. There's no right or wrong choice as long as it's something that helps you to move on without getting stuck thinking about how things didn't go your way.

↳ **5. Look Ahead:** Write down three things you're excited about in your future. They can be about your entrepreneurial journey or anything else you're looking forward to.

Try to remember that it's normal to feel disappointed when things don't go as planned, but don't let that stop you from moving forward!

Chapter 3:

THE POWER OF MENTORSHIP: LEARNING FROM THE BEST

The more you know,
the more you grow.

SOFIA
Sofia the First

WHAT IS MENTORSHIP AND WHY IS IT IMPORTANT?

Think about the last time you learned something new. Maybe it was cooking, painting, or coding. You didn't know everything at first, right? But with the help of someone more experienced, like your dad or mom showing you how to make your favorite cookies, or a teacher guiding you through an art project, you learned faster. That's mentorship.

A mentor is a person more experienced in a particular area who is willing to share their knowledge with you. In the world of entrepreneurship, mentors often have successful businesses of their own and have faced challenges you're probably going to come up against. They can provide guidance, support, encouragement, save you from making mistakes, and even open doors to new opportunities.

A mentor can help you feel more confident about trying new things and making important decisions. Just like a coach in sports, a mentor can help you see your strengths and where you need to do some work. The most successful entrepreneurs have all had mentors to guide them along the way.

HOW TO FIND A MENTOR

→ **Know What You Need:** Before you start looking for a mentor, you need to know what you want to learn from them. Are you looking for information on how to start a business, how to deal with customers, or how to balance school and business? Knowing what you need will help you find the right person to guide you.

→ **Look Around You:** Start with the people you know. This could be a teacher, a family friend who runs a business, or a community member you admire. If they can't be your mentor, they might be able to introduce you to someone who can.

→ **Reach Out to Local Businesses:** Visit local businesses that are doing what want to do and ask if the owner or manager would be willing to talk to you about their experiences. Be polite, explain why you're interested, and ask if they would be open to mentoring you. Get the permission of a parent or guardian before you go off talking to strangers, though.

Once you find a potential mentor:

→ **Be Genuine:** Explain why you're reaching out to them, what you hope to learn, and why you think they'd be a good mentor. Be honest and sincere.

→ **Be Respectful:** Respect their time and expertise. Make sure to prepare for any meetings you have with them by having your questions ready in advance. Remember that no one owes you anything. So when a mentor shares their expertise, be sure to pay attention, and take notes as a sign of respect and so that you don't need to go back to ask the same questions again.

→ **Be Appreciative:** Always thank them for their time and advice. Even if someone can't be your mentor, they might give you valuable tips and contacts.

→ **Be Patient:** Building a relationship with a mentor takes time.

Remember, finding a mentor is not about finding the most successful entrepreneur out there. It's about finding someone who believes in you, understands your goals, and is willing to help you grow.

BELLA'S
BATH BOMBS

Bella had always loved making things. From baking cookies with her mom to crafting origami with her friends, she loved using her hands and her imagination to create something new. One day, while using a bath bomb she had received as a gift, she thought, "I wonder if I could make these myself?"

So, she did her research, learned the science behind the fizz, and made her very first bath bomb. It was a simple lavender-scented bath bomb, but to Bella it was a masterpiece. She made more and gave them to her friends, and, to her surprise, they absolutely loved them!

Seeing a potential business opportunity, Bella decided to start selling her bath bombs. She quickly realized that running a business was not as simple as making a product. There was so much she didn't know.

So, Bella's mother introduced her to Mrs. Martinez, a family friend who owned a successful handmade lotion business. Bella sent Mrs. Martinez an email explaining

her business and things she needed help with and asked if Mrs. Martinez would be willing to be her mentor. Bella impressed Mrs. Martinez so she agreed to help.

Over the next few months, Bella and Mrs. Martinez met regularly to discuss Bella's list of questions, and Mrs. Martinez taught Bella important lessons about entrepreneurship.

Bella learned how to price her products, how to create pretty packaging that stood out, and how to find customers to buy her bath bombs. Mrs. Martinez also encouraged Bella to believe in herself and remember that success comes from hard work and not giving up. Eventually Bella's bath bomb business really took off at local craft fairs and online through her new website. The whole process would have been so much harder if Bella hadn't found a mentor.

SUGGESTED ACTIVITY: REACH OUT To PoTENTIAL MENToRS

Now it's your turn! Here is a fun activity for you.

INSTRUCTIONS

Identify Potential Mentors: First, think about the people you know who might be willing to mentor you. They might be:

- Business owners in your neighborhood or community.

- Teachers, tutors or coaches.

- Friends of your parents or older siblings.

- Community leaders.

- Authors, speakers, or influencers who inspire you.
  (**You can reach out to them online but remember to be safe and always involve your parents when contacting people online.**)

- **Make a List:** Write the names of these potential mentors and a little bit about why you think they could help you. Are they experienced in a field you're interested in? Do they seem smart and supportive? Have they done something that you would like to do someday?

- **Write a Letter:** Choose one person from your list and write them a letter. Introduce yourself, tell them about your interests, and explain why you're looking for a mentor. Let them know why you think they would be a good mentor for you and politely ask if they would consider it.

- **Send Your Letter:** Send your letter. It can be a physical letter or an email. As you wait for their answer, remember that it's okay if they say no or don't respond at all. The important thing is that you took the chance and asked.

- **Reflect:** After you've sent your letter, write in your journal about this experience. How did it feel to ask someone to be your mentor? What did you learn from this activity? Finding a mentor might take time, but it will be worth it in the end.

SAMPLE LETTER TO POTENTIAL MENTOR

Dear [*Potential Mentor's Name*],

My name is [*Your Name*], and I am a 10-year-old with big dreams and a passion for entrepreneurship. I am writing this letter to introduce myself, share my interests, and express my excitement about the possibility of having you as a mentor.

Ever since I can remember, I have been fascinated by the world of business and the idea of starting my own small business. I love coming up with creative ideas and finding innovative solutions to problems. From running a lemonade stand in my neighborhood to organizing mini events with my friends, I have always enjoyed the thrill of creating something and watching it grow.

I am reaching out to you because I truly admire your achievements and expertise in the business field. Your entrepreneurial journey and success inspire me, and I believe that your guidance and wisdom would be invaluable as I start my own small business venture.

Your experience and knowledge in [*mention a specific area of expertise or industry related to the mentor*] make you an ideal mentor for me. I have been following your work and have been impressed by your innovative ideas, leadership skills, and dedication. I believe that your guidance and mentorship can help me navigate the challenges and make the right decisions along my entrepreneurial journey.

Having a mentor like you would not only provide me with valuable insights and advice but also give me the confidence to pursue my dreams. Your support and guidance would mean the world to me as I take my first steps into the business world.

I understand that your time is valuable, and I would be grateful for any guidance or mentorship you can offer. If you would be open to being my mentor, I would be thrilled to learn from you, discuss my ideas and seek your advice.

Thank you for considering my request, and I hope to hear from you soon. I am excited about the possibility of having you as my mentor and the opportunity to learn from your expertise.

Warm regards,

[*Your Name*]

Chapter 4:

BUSINESS BASICS: UNDERSTANDING MONEY MATTERS

The question isn't
who's going to let me,
it's who's going to stop me.

AYN RAND
Author, and Philosopher

OK, WE ARE ABOUT TO GET INTO ONE OF THE MOST EXCITING PARTS OF RUNNING A BUSINESS - MONEY! WE'RE NOT JUST TALKING ABOUT THE MONEY YOU EARN, BUT ALSO THE MONEY YOU SPEND TO KEEP YOUR BUSINESS UP AND RUNNING.

THIS IS WHAT WE CALL 'BUSINESS FINANCE'.

So, what is business finance? Well, it's all about how money flows in and out of your business and that's called cash flow. This includes everything from the first money you use to start your business, to the money you spend on supplies and expenses, to the money you earn from selling your products or services.

The money you earn from your business is your "income" or "revenue" – that's the money you make from selling your awesome products or services. The money you spend to buy supplies, advertise or pay a helper is "expense". The goal is to make more money than you spend, or to have more income than expense.

Remember Julien's Lemonade Stand from Chapter 1? The money Julien spent on lemons, sugar, and cups were her expenses. When Sara sold a cup of lemonade, the money she earned was her income. If Julien earned more from selling lemonade than she spent on supplies, she made a "profit." Profit is the money that's left over after all the expenses are paid.

Here are important terms to know:

↳ **Profit:** The difference between what you spend and what you earn is your profit:

Sara's Lemonade Stand sells each cup of lemonade for $1.00, and it costs 60 cents to make each cup of lemonade (lemons, sugar, cup).

Selling Price (revenue) – Selling Cost (expenses) = Profit

$1.00 – 60 cents = 40 cents Profit

So...for each cup of lemonade Sara sells, she earns a profit of forty cents. It might seem like a small amount but imagine if she sells one hundred cups in a day - that's $40 in profit! Over time, those forty cents add up.

↳ **Earnings:** This is another word for the money you make from selling your products or services. Keep track of your earnings so you can see how your business is doing. If your earnings are going up, that's a good sign your business is growing.

Loss: A loss happens when your expenses are more than your income. For example, if Sara spent more money on lemons, sugar, and cups than she made from selling lemonade, she would have a loss. A loss is not a good thing, but it happens sometimes, especially when a business is new. It's important to learn from a loss and try to make changes so that it doesn't happen again.

Budgeting: A budget is a plan for how you'll spend your money. It helps you think ahead to be sure you're not spending more than you're earning. You can have a budget for your business and a budget for yourself and it's easy to do.

On a piece of paper, on the left side of the page list all the money you expect to earn or receive during a period of time like a week or a month. Then on the right-hand side of the page, list all the things you plan to spend money on during that same time period. Add up the money coming in, add up the money going out. If you have more coming in than going out, you're in good shape. If not, you will need to either figure out how to bring in more money or reduce the amount of money going out.

Remember Julien's Lemonade Stand? Let's say Julien expected to earn $100 selling lemonade in July. She also expects to pay $15 for lemon, $20 for sugar, and $25 for cups. Julien also wants to save $40. So that's:

$100-$15-$20-$25-$40= $0. Julien budgeted for all the money she expected to earn in July.

Record Keeping: It's important to keep track of all the money coming in and going out of your business. You can use a simple notebook, or a computer spreadsheet, to record all your income and expenses, no matter how small. Keeping track will make it easier to figure out if you have enough money to invest or to save.

Pricing: How you price your products or services is important. Price too high, and customers may not buy. Price too low, and you might not make a profit. To set the right price, you'll need to know your costs and understand what customers are willing to pay. We will dig deeper into pricing in later chapters.

Loans: Sometimes, you might need to borrow money to start or grow your business, maybe for a new lemonade stand or an ice machine. This is a "loan." A loan is money that you borrow and promise to pay back, usually with an extra amount called "interest." The person or company who lends you the money charges you interest as a fee for letting you use their money. Be careful when considering a loan. It's important to know how and when you'll pay it back, and how much interest it will cost you.

➥ **Supply and Demand:** These two terms are fundamental in understanding how a market works. Demand refers to how many people want the product you're selling. Supply refers to how much of that product you must sell. If there's high demand for your product and low supply, you might be able to charge more for it. But if there's low demand and high supply, you may have to lower your prices to encourage people to buy. For example, if it's a sweltering summer day, more people will want to buy lemonade (high demand), and if you only have a few cups left (low supply), you might decide to charge a bit more. Likewise, if customers aren't interested in lemonade because it's not that hot and you have several pitchers of lemonade on hand, then there's low demand and high supply so you might consider reducing your price.

➥ **Inventory:** This is the amount of product that you have on hand to sell. If Julien makes a big batch of lemonade in the morning, her inventory is all the cups of lemonade she has ready to sell. It's important to manage your inventory well - if you make too much lemonade and don't sell it all, you could lose money. But if you don't make enough and run out, you could lose sales.

➥ **Break-Even Point:** This is the point at which your total revenue (money coming in from sales) equals your total costs (money going out for expenses). In other words, it's the point where you're not making a profit, but you're not losing money either. Knowing your break-even point can help you set your prices and plan your sales. For example, if it costs Sara $60 to make one hundred cups of lemonade, she needs to sell at least 100 cups for $1 each to reach her break-even point.

➥ **Investing:** A smart entrepreneur knows that to grow a business, sometimes you must put the money you earn back into the business. This is 'investing' or 'reinvesting.' Let's say that in August Julien decided to use some of her profits to buy tea so she could add iced tea to her menu, and she decided to print flyers to advertise around the neighborhood, and to buy a lemonade dispenser so she could pour lemonade faster. Each of these expenses would help her earn more money so they would be good investments.

↪ **Saving:** Saving money is important for everyone, not just entrepreneurs. When you save a part of your income you can be prepared for unexpected expenses like buying more supplies when your business gets popular, or replacing the tire on your bike if it gets a hole in it. Saving is also important for your future goals. Maybe you want to buy a skateboard this year or pay for college when you get older. If you spend all the money that you earn, you won't be able to reach your goals. We'll talk about ways to save your money in a little bit.

MOLLY AND ELLA'S SWEET TEETH

When sisters Molly and Ella were just 10 and 11 years old, they discovered a shared passion for creating sweet treats. They often experimented in the kitchen, inventing new candy flavors that their friends and family couldn't get enough of. The idea for 'Sweet Tooth Delights' sprouted from positive feedback they got from their taste-testers.

Turning their passion into a business wasn't easy. They needed ingredients, packaging materials, and a place to sell their candies.

So, they sat down and listed their startup costs which included ingredients like sugar, food coloring, flavor extracts, and costs for packaging the treats and renting a booth at a weekend farmers market. They estimated their startup costs to be $150. To raise this amount, they saved their allowances, did extra chores, and held a yard sale.

Once they had the money to get started, they began making their candies in larger batches and opened their stall at the local market. Each candy sold for more than it cost them to make, so they knew they were earning a profit, but they didn't just spend it all. They practiced smart money habits.

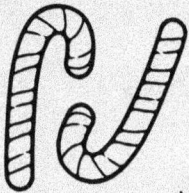

Part of what they earned was used to cover their weekly costs like replacing the ingredients. They saved some to reinvest in the company like when they decided to start making lollipops to earn more money. Some was set aside for unexpected events like when their candy thermometer broke and they had to buy a new one.

The girls kept a record of all their sales and expenses in a notebook. This helped them track their profits, identify best-selling flavors, and even notice that sales were higher on sunny days!

By budgeting, saving, and investing, Molly and Mia turned their small candy stall into a success, with customers eagerly waiting for their new candy flavors.

Chapter 5:

YOUR BUSINESS PLAN - ROADMAP TO SUCCESS

You can't be that kid standing
at the top of the water slide,
overthinking it.
You have to go down the chute.

TINA FEY, ACTRESS
Comedian, and Writer

NOW IT'S TIME TO PUT YOUR IDEAS INTO ACTION BY CREATING A BUSINESS PLAN. A BUSINESS PLAN IS LIKE A ROADMAP. YOU WRITE YOUR GOALS, AND THE STEPS YOU'LL HAVE TO TAKE TO GET TO YOUR GOALS. IT DOESN'T HAVE TO BE COMPLICATED, AND YOU DON'T NEED TO SPEND A LONG TIME MAKING IT, BUT IF YOU DON'T HAVE ONE, CHANCES ARE YOU'RE GOING TO GET LOST.

BE PREPARED TO BE FLEXIBLE AS WELL. WHEN YOUR IDEAS OR GOALS CHANGE, SO WILL YOUR BUSINESS PLAN.

In this chapter, we'll dive into what goes into a business plan. We'll use examples and a sample plan for a dog walking business to help you understand how to write one for your own business.

WHY IS A BUSINESS PLAN IMPORTANT?

↳ **Get Clear on Your Goals:** A business plan helps you spell out your business idea, why you're doing it, and where you see your company going in the future, including who you hope to help or serve. This is how you let other people know your plan.

↳ **Pick Your Customers:** A business plan helps you decide who your customers are (your target market). It also helps you figure out how you're going to get your target market to buy from you, and come back again and again.

↳ **Plan Your Finances:** A business plan helps you estimate the costs involved in starting and running your business. It also helps you estimate how much money you're likely to earn.

↳ **Make Decisions**: A business plan holds most of the information you'll need to make important decisions about your business, like what kind of marketing you should do, what you need to keep the business running, and what it will take to help your business grow.

To give you an example of how to put together a business plan, let's look at a dog walking business. We'll walk through the suggested sections of the plan and then show you a sample Business Plan. This is just a guide. You can change it to fit your business idea.

→ 1. **Executive Summary:** Write a brief description of your dog walking business, including your goals for now and the future.

→ 2. **Business Description:** Describe your dog walking services, including the part of town you serve, the types of dogs you'll walk, and any additional services you plan to offer, like pet sitting or dog training.

→ 3. **Market Analysis**: Research who you think might need your services. Are there busy professionals or older people who need help with their pets? Is anyone else offering dog walking services?

→ 4. **Organization and Management:** If you plan to work with a team, write down who will be doing what and describe any experience the other team members have. Has anyone on the team walked dogs before? Has anyone taken any training classes like obedience school?

→ 5. **Services:** Describe your dog walking services, including how long the walks will be, whether you'll walk more than one dog at a time, and any special care

you'll provide for certain breeds or special needs dogs.

→ 6. **Marketing and Sales Strategy**: Explain how you'll advertise your services to get clients. This could include things like creating a website, putting a post on a neighborhood chat, distributing flyers, or partnering with local pet stores or veterinarians.

→ 7. **How Much You Think You'll Earn:** Estimate your startup costs, your monthly expenses, and how much you're going to charge. Estimate how many dog walks you expect to complete each month and multiply that number by the dollar amount you plan to charge for each walk. That total will be your estimated income. Add up all the things you expect to have to pay for during the month and those are your expenses. The difference between your income and your expenses is your financial projection, or the amount you expect to earn.

→ 8. **Funding Request:** If you need money to get started, include the amount you're looking for and explain how it will be used to grow your business.

→ 9. **Appendix**: This is the extra section where you can include things like any certifications or training you've completed, licenses required for operating a dog walking business in your area, and positive written statements from satisfied clients, if you have any.

Here's a sample Business Plan for a dog walking business:

KADEN'S DOGGIE WALKS
BUSINESS PLAN

↳ **Executive Summary:** Doggie Walks is a professional dog walking service that provides reliable and compassionate care for furry friends in the downtown area. My mission is to ensure the well-being and happiness of dogs while giving their owners peace of mind. As an experienced dog walker, I am committed to offering exceptional service and building lasting relationships with both pets and their owners.

↳ **Business Description**: Doggie Walks will offer daily dog walking services. We will serve busy professionals and individuals who require assistance in caring for their dogs. Our services will include 30-minute walks. We will offer additional services such as feeding, providing fresh drinking water, and basic grooming.

↳ **Market Analysis:** The downtown area has a high concentration of dog owners who are often busy with work and other commitments. Many of them feel guilty leaving their pets alone for extended periods. Doggie Walks aims to fill this gap by providing reliable and professional dog walking services. The demand for such services is high, and we think we will do well.

↳ **Organization and Management:** Doggie Walks is owned and operated by Kaden, a lifelong dog lover with experience in pet care. Kaden will oversee the day-to-day operations and perform all the walks, manage client relationships, and ensure the highest quality of care.

- **Services:** Our services include daily walks, and personalized care for dogs with special requirements. We prioritize safety, exercise, and providing a positive experience for every furry friend.

- **Marketing and Sales Strategy:** To promote our services, we will create a user-friendly website with detailed information about our walks and pricing, and testimonials from satisfied clients. We will also use the local neighborhood chat to reach our target audience and showcase our commitment to animal welfare. Additionally, we will distribute flyers in the neighborhood to advertise the business and offer special promotions.

- **Financial Projections:** Based on market research and projected growth, we estimate our startup costs to be $100 to be used to create a simple website and print flyers. Our pricing will be competitive, with a rate of $15 for a 30-minute walk. We anticipate steady growth in our client base, with an average of 5 walks per day in the first year. With this projection, we expect to achieve profitability, by earning more than we've spent, within the first year of operation.

- **Funding Request:** We are seeking funding of $100 to cover our initial startup costs, including marketing materials and website.

- **Appendix:**
  - Certifications and training completed
  - References from satisfied clients

- **Conclusion:** Doggie Walks is ready to meet the growing demand for professional dog walking services in the downtown area. With a focus on exceptional care, reliability, and customer satisfaction, we are confident that our business will be successful and be helpful for dogs and their owners.

Chapter 6

HOW TO GET MONEY TO START YOUR BUSINESS OR KEEP IT RUNNING

You're braver than you believe,
and stronger than you see,
and smarter than you think.

CHRISTOPHER ROBIN
Winnie the Pooh

IF YOU'RE LUCKY, YOUR BUSINESS DOESN'T REQUIRE ANY MONEY TO GET STARTED, BUT AT SOME POINT, EVERY BUSINESS WILL NEED MONEY SO IT'S IMPORTANT TO HAVE SOME IDEAS ABOUT HOW TO GET IT.

First, take the time to figure out how much money you're going to need and write it down. Before considering other sources, think about whether you can earn money doing extra chores or from a part-time job. If you're going to need more money than you can earn on your own, here are some other ideas:

↪ **Personal Savings:** This is money that you have saved up over time from things like allowances and birthday money.

↪ **Loans:** This is money you borrow and are expected to pay back.

As a young entrepreneur, your best bet for getting a loan will be from your parents or a family member. If they agree, then write down how much they are willing to loan you, when they expect you to pay them back, and how often they expect you to make payments. If they are charging you interest, make sure to write that down, too.

> ***Interest* is an extra amount that can be added onto loans to pay the lender for using their money.**

Both you and your parent or family member should sign the agreement so that there is no confusion in the future. When you borrow money, even if it's from your parents, it is your responsibility to pay back the loan on time and in full.

As your business grows, you can start to research options such as traditional bank loans, or microloans for small businesses. You will fill out an application, pay interest, and make payments. You'll have to write a detailed business plan explaining how you'll use the loan. But for now, we will keep it simple.

↪ **Grants and Competitions:** A grant is money given away by an organization for a particular purpose. There are organizations that offer grants for young entrepreneurs. This is money you don't have to pay back!

There are also competitions where you can win money for your business.

Research grants and competitions for young entrepreneurs online or go to our website at HTTPS://THEBOLDESTMEKIDS.COM

Crowdfunding: This is when you raise money from many people usually using an online platform. You explain your business idea and ask people to donate money to help you get started. In return, you can offer them special perks or rewards, like a product from your business once it's up and running.

While it can be a great way to see what kind of interest there is in your product or service, it can take a lot of time and effort.

Raising money requires planning and creativity. You might need to get money from more than one place.

RIYA'S
TERRIFIC TEES

Riya, a 14-year-old student, had always had an eye for design. She was good at spotting fashion trends and talented at graphic design, so she decided to use her skills to start a t-shirt design business.

But starting a business wasn't easy for Riya. She faced some big challenges. One major obstacle was the cost. As a teenager with limited funds, Riya had to find a way to afford the screen-printing equipment, high-quality blank t-shirts, and design software. And that wasn't all! She also had to think about the ongoing expenses like paying for a website, shipping products, and buying new materials.

To tackle these financial hurdles, Riya came up with a few smart strategies. She decided to start small and invest her own money instead of looking for outside funding. She bought a used screen printing machine and just enough blank shirts for her first few orders. Riya also kept her costs down by using free design software online and a printing service that only charged her for the number of shirts she had orders for (print-on-demand) so she didn't have to pay for lots of shirts to be printed at once.

Managing her cash flow was another important lesson for Riya. She learned the value of budgeting by carefully keeping track of her income and every expense. From the cost of the T-shirts to the price she sold them for, she recorded everything to understand how her money was being spent. Riya even set aside a portion of her profits for unexpected costs, so she was prepared for any surprises.

Riya overcame her initial financial challenges, and "Terrific Tees" became a big hit in her local community, showing everyone that age is no barrier to success.

NATALIE'S
PLANET-SAVING BEES

Natalie was 12-year-old who had a deep love for nature and the environment. As she explored different ways to contribute to the well-being of the planet, she discovered the importance of bees and their role in our ecosystem.

Natalie noticed that her community didn't have local honey which meant that there must not be enough bees in her community. It was important to Natalie to support the bee populations, so she decided to start a beekeeping business and provide her community with locally sourced, pure, and sustainable honey while also promoting the importance of bee conservation.

To bring her vision to life, Natalie needed funds to buy beehives, beekeeping equipment, protective gear, and an

online course about beekeeping. Since her parents were unable to help her fund her business, Natalie had to find creative ways to finance it.

To make money, Natalie started babysitting part-time. Once she earned enough to launch her beekeeping business, she soon expanded her product line to include not only honey but other bee-related products such as beeswax candles, beeswax wraps, and natural skincare products made with honey and beeswax. She teamed up with local artists who shared her commitment to sustainability and advertised their products with her honey which helped her sell more of her own products.

Natalie educated her community about the importance of bees and the need to protect their habitats. She gave talks at local elementary schools, and organized workshops for kids.

Natalie's role as a young beekeeper taught her valuable lessons about entrepreneurship, responsibility, and environmental stewardship.

SUGGESTED ACTIVITY: PITCHING TO YOUR PARENTS OR FAMILY MEMBER

When you pitch an idea, you explain it to other people so that they understand what you do, why you need money, and what you plan to do with that money. A pitch should be both informative and interesting. Have you ever had someone try to sell you something? If they don't explain what they're selling very well, or if they don't seem very excited about it, you're probably not going to buy anything.

While it may seem a little scary, presenting your business idea to your parents or other family members can be a great way to develop your pitch, and you might get money to start your business.

INSTRUCTIONS

Step 1: Prepare Your Business Plan

Before you can pitch your idea, you need to fully understand your own business plan. This means knowing your product or service, target audience, marketing strategy, pricing model, and financial projections.

Step 2: Develop Your Elevator Pitch

An elevator pitch is a brief speech that you can use to get people interested in what you're doing. It's called an elevator pitch because it should only be as long as it takes to ride an elevator with someone. It should be brief, clear, and interesting. Try to cover what you do, how you do it, and why you do it in a couple of sentences.

Step 3: Anticipate Questions

Think about the questions your parents or family members might ask and have answers ready. They may ask about risks, how much you expect to earn, your competition, or how you plan to balance school and business.

Step 4: Practice Your Pitch

Rehearse your pitch until you're comfortable presenting it. Practice with a friend or record yourself.

Step 5: The Pitch

Arrange a meeting time with your parents or family members, dress neatly or even professionally and present your pitch.

Step 6: Handle Feedback

Be open to feedback. Remember that your parents or family members want the best for you and any feedback they give is to help you improve.

At the end of the activity, think about what you learned. Did you feel confident while presenting? What questions were hard to answer? What would you do differently next time?

Chapter 7:

PRICING AND COSTS

The more that you read,
the more things you will know.
The more that you learn,
the more places you will go.

DR. SEUSS
Oh the Places You'll Go!

NEXT, LET'S DIVE INTO A TOPIC THAT CAN SEEM A LITTLE TRICKY AT FIRST, BUT IS SUPER IMPORTANT WHEN YOU'RE RUNNING A BUSINESS: PRICING YOUR PRODUCT OR SERVICE.

BUT BEFORE WE EVEN THINK ABOUT WHAT PRICE TO SET, WE NEED TO UNDERSTAND THE COST OF GOODS AND SERVICES.

Everything that goes into making your product or providing your service—craft materials, ingredients for a cookie recipe, or even just the time you spend—has a cost attached to it. In business we call this the cost of goods sold (or COGS for short).

Let's say you're making and selling homemade candles. The cost of the wax, wick, dye, fragrance, jars, and labels all add up to your COGS. Plus, don't forget about the time you spend making them. Your time is valuable!

Now, if you're providing a service, like dog walking or tutoring, the cost might be different. Instead of materials, you might be spending more on transportation to get to your clients' homes, or on educational materials, or dog treats. And again, don't forget about the value of your time!

So, to figure out what your costs are, you'll make a list of everything you use and how much of it you use for each item or service. Once you know how much you're spending, you can think about how to set your prices. Let's try an example:

MEG'S
GIFT BASKETS

Meg creates and sells beautiful gift baskets filled with all sorts of lovely treats. Some baskets have snacks while others have lotions and soaps, and still others have toys or candies and cookies. When Meg buys items to go in her baskets, she keeps a record of the cost. So, if she buys 10 candy bars for a total of $10, she knows that each candy bar costs $1. If she buys a decorative box of cookies for $5, she adds that to her list of costs. She buys plastic grass to decorate her baskets and each bag costs $1. She buys baskets that cost $4 each.

So, when Meg decides to make a gift basket that includes 3 candy bars and 2 boxes of cookies, one bag of plastic grass and a basket, all she has to do is look at her list of purchased items to calculate her costs.

Candy bars = $_____

Cookies = $_____

Grass = $_____

Basket = $_____

Total Cost = $_____

> If Meg wants to earn money when she sells her basket, she will need to price it higher than the amount it costs to make it.

When it comes to setting prices, the first rule is that your price should always be more than your cost. Why? Because the difference between the price you charge, and your cost is your profit, and the goal of a business, among other things, is to earn a profit.

The second rule is to think about what your customers are willing to pay. For instance, if you're selling handcrafted bracelets, and the materials cost you $5 per bracelet, and it takes you half an hour to make one, you could try to sell them for $20. This way, you're not just covering your costs, but also getting paid for your time and effort.

But what if the other kids in your neighborhood are only willing to pay $10 for a bracelet? This is where market research comes in. Look around and see what products or services like yours are selling for. Ask your potential customers how much they would be willing to pay.

Remember, there's no one 'right' price. Your price might change over time as you get more skilled, as the cost of your materials goes up or down, or as you learn more about what your customers care about. Pricing is something you'll get better at with practice.

PRICING STRATEGIES

Now that you've got the hang of setting your prices to cover your costs and make a profit, let's look at different pricing strategies:

↳ **Cost-plus Pricing:** This is what we've been talking about so far. You figure out how much it costs you to make your product or provide your service, then add a bit more to make a profit. This is an easy and fair way to price, and it's a great place to start.

- **Competitive Pricing:** This is when you set your prices based on what other businesses (your competition) are charging for the same types of products or services. If everyone else is selling handmade bracelets for $10, you might want to price yours around the same amount, or a little less.

- **Value-based Pricing:** This is when you set your prices based on the value your product or service provides to the customer. For example, if you're offering pet sitting services and you provide extra value (like giving the pets a bath or teaching them new tricks), you might be able to charge more than someone who just feeds and walks the pets.

- **Psychological Pricing:** Ever wondered why so many prices end in .99 or .95? It's because studies have shown that we think of $4.99 as being a lot less than $5.00, even though the difference is just a penny! So if everyone else is selling bracelets for $10, you could sell yours for $9.99.

The strategy you choose should depend on your business, your costs, your competition, and your customers. Try out different strategies and see what works best for you. And always be ready to adjust your prices as things change.

TO DISCOUNT OR NOT TO DISCOUNT: THE PROS AND CONS OF SALES PROMOTIONS

Deals like '50% OFF' or 'Buy One, Get One Free' can be exciting, but should you use them for your business?

PROS

- **Attract More Customers:** A discount can make your product or service more attractive to customers who might think your regular price is too high.

- **Clear Out Old Products You Haven't Sold:** The products that you have that are ready to be sold are called inventory. If you have too much inventory that you don't think you can sell, that's known as excess inventory. Sometimes it makes sense to give customers a discount so that you sell the excess inventory more quickly and move on to selling other products.

- **Holiday Sales:** Special occasions like Christmas, Thanksgiving, or even the anniversary of your business can be great times to offer sales promotions.

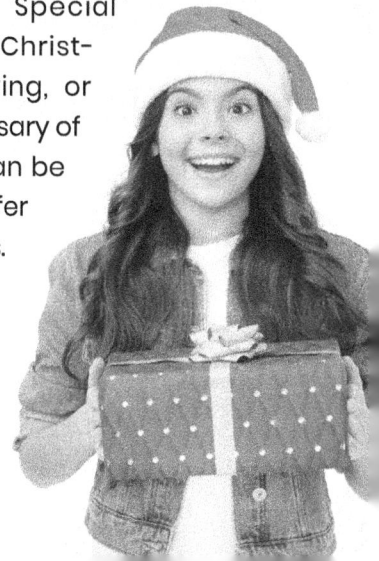

CONS

↳ **Customers Might Not Value Products on Sale:** If your products or services are always on sale, people might start to think they're not worth the original price.

↳ **Profit:** Sales promotions might attract more customers, but you'll also earn less profit on each sale.

↳ **Short-term Customers:** Sometimes discounts attract customers who are only interested in the deal, not in your product or service itself. They might not become repeat customers once the sale is over and one of the best ways to grow your business is to have repeat customers.

So, should you offer discounts and sales promotions? It depends! They can be great toosl when you use them at the right times and for the right reasons. Like everything in entrepreneurship, it's about finding a balance and testing different strategies.

ZOE'S
ENCHANTED GARDENS

Zoe, a creative and ambitious 12-year-old, had a passion for creating whimsical miniature fairy gardens. The more gardens she designed, the more compliments she got from friends and family, so she decided to start a business selling them, and Zoe's Enchanted Gardens was born.

Zoe knew that pricing her miniature fairy gardens would be an important part of getting customers to buy them and making sure that the business would be profitable. She started by adding up the cost of materials, the time it took to make each garden, and the demand for her unique product.

Competitive Analysis: Zoe went online to research how other businesses selling fairy gardens were pricing their products.

Discounts and Promotions: She recognized the importance of attracting new customers and getting sales from her old customers. So, she used different pricing methods, including discounts and promotions. Zoe offered introductory discounts to new customers, giving them a lower price for their first purchase. She also ran promotions during holiday seasons. These deals helped build excitement and encouraged customers to buy.

Options: Zoe created different products for different types of customers. She sold DIY kits at lower prices for people who wanted the experience of creating their own fairy gardens. She also designed custom gardens specially made for each customer and sold them at higher prices.

Upselling and Cross-selling: When customers purchased a fairy garden kit, Zoe recommended little people and animal figurines that went with the theme of the garden. Selling customers additional products that improve the original purchase is called upselling. Zoe also sold additional garden scenes like ponds and waterfalls and barns. Selling customers products that don't necessarily go with the original purchase but are related is called cross-selling. Both strategies helped her earn more money and kept her customers coming back for more.

Building Customer Loyalty: She started a customer rewards program. For every purchase, customers earned points that could be used to get discounts on future purchases. This encouraged repeat business.

Continuous Improvement: Zoe regularly reviewed and adjusted her pricing strategies based on customer feedback, paying attention to how other fairy garden creators were pricing their products, and making sure that her pricing covered her costs.

SUGGESTED ACTIVITY: THE PRICING GAME

OBJECTIVE

Learn how to price your product or service by considering costs, competition, and value to the customer.

MATERIALS

Pen, paper, calculator, internet access for research

INSTRUCTIONS

↳ **1. Define your product or service:** Write down what you plan to sell as a part of your business. If you already have a business, choose one product or service you offer.

↳ **2. Identify your costs:** List all the costs of creating your product or offering your service. Remember to include material costs, packaging, your time, and any other costs.

↳ **3. Calculate the total cost:** Add up all the costs you've listed. This is how much it costs you to make one product or offer one service.

↳ **4. Research your competitors:** Search the internet to find out how much other businesses are charging for similar products or services. List at least three examples.

↳ **5. Set your initial price:** Based on your costs and what your competitors are charging, decide on a price for your product or service.

↳ **6. Test your price:** Show your product or service (or a description of it) to friends or family members. Tell them the price you've decided on. Do they think it's a good price? Would they pay that much for it? Why or why not?

↳ **7. Reflect and revise:** Based on the feedback you've received, consider whether you need to adjust your price. Remember, a great price covers your costs, is competitive, and feels like good value to your customers.

↳ **8. Journal about your experience:** What did you learn from this activity? How did it feel to price your product or service? What surprised you? What will you do differently next time?

Chapter 8:

THE LEGAL STUFF AND TAXES MADE SIMPLE

Why, sometimes I've believed as many as six impossible things before breakfast.

LEWIS CARROLL
Alice's Adventures in Wonderland

WHAT'S A LEGAL STRUCTURE?

As we dive deeper into the world of business, there's an important topic we need to talk about: legal structures. This might sound complicated, but we'll just give you an overview.

In the simplest terms, a legal structure refers to how a business is organized and operated. This affects everything from how much tax you pay to the paperwork you need to file, and even how much financial responsibility (also called liability) you have if something goes wrong with your business. As your business grows, you and your parents or guardians will talk with accountants or lawyers to help you decide what structure to use, but for now, the most common legal structure for a brand-new entrepreneur with a small business is **sole proprietorship**.

This is the simplest structure. If you're the sole proprietor, it means that you're the only person running the show. You make all the decisions, but you also take on all the legal and financial responsibility. This can be a good place to start for young entrepreneurs and a good fit for your new business.

Other legal structures include partnerships, corporations, limited liability corporations (LLCs) and combinations of these structures. For now, however, we will assume that you will be using sole proprietorship for your new business.

WHAT DO I NEED TO KNOW ABOUT TAXES?

It's important to understand what taxes are and how they affect your business. Taxes are a way for the government to collect money to pay for public services like schools, roads, and healthcare. When you earn money through your business, you may need to pay taxes on that income.

In fact, anyone who is self-employed and earns $400 a year or more must file a tax return, and there's no minimum age.

TYPES OF TAXES

There are different types of taxes that you may come across as an entrepreneur. As your business grows, you and your parents may need to work with an accountant to help you with taxes, but for now, the two main types are income taxes and sales taxes:

→ **Income Taxes:** Income taxes are taxes paid on the money you earn. The specific rules for reporting and paying income taxes may be different depending on where you live, but in general, the form you fill out, called an income tax return, tells the government how much money you earned and how much tax you need to pay.

When you earn money, like when you have a job or run a business, the government wants to make sure that everyone pays their fair share of taxes. It's important to fill out your tax return accurately and on time. As a young person, you might not have to file a tax return if you don't earn much money or if you're still dependent on your parents. It's always a good idea to ask a trusted adult or a tax professional for help if you're unsure about what to do.

Filing a tax return might seem a little confusing at first, but it's an important part of being a responsible citizen. It helps ensure that everyone contributes their fair share to the community, and it's a way to support the things that make our country better for everyone.

→ **Sales Taxes:** These are taxes added to the price of goods or services that you sell. When you make a sale, you may need to collect sales tax from your customers and send it to the government. The rules for sales taxes vary depending on where you live.

As we've already mentioned, it's important to keep track of all the money you earn from sales and any costs or expenses related to your business, such as supplies, equipment, or advertising. This information will be helpful when it's time to fill out your tax forms.

We will cover more advanced legal and tax topics in the next book, including:

→ Partnerships, corporations, limited liability corporations (LLCs)

→ Estimated taxes

→ Trademarks, and copyrights, and logos...oh MY!

For now, just remember that when it comes to legal matters and taxes, it's always best to talk with a professional.

Chapter 9

MARKETING: HOW TO LET PEOPLE KNOW ABOUT YOUR AWESOME PRODUCT OR SERVICE

If you can dream it,
you can do it.

WALT DISNEY

HAVE YOU EVER BEEN WALKING THROUGH A STORE AND SEEN A BRIGHT, COLORFUL DISPLAY THAT CAUGHT YOUR EYE AND MADE YOU WANT TO KNOW MORE ABOUT THE PRODUCT? HAVE YOU SEEN AN AD ON TV FOR A COOL NEW GADGET THAT YOU JUST COULDN'T WAIT TO TRY? THESE ARE EXAMPLES OF MARKETING IN ACTION.

Marketing, in simple terms, is the way businesses let people know about their products or services. It's a little like waving a big, sparkly sign that says, "Hey, check this out! Isn't it amazing?" But instead of a sign, you might use a catchy jingle, an appealing image, a fun video, or an exciting event.

Marketing is incredibly important for any entrepreneur because no matter how amazing your product or service might be, if no one knows about it, you can't make any sales. And without sales, you don't have a business.

There are all types of marketing. Here are some examples:

↳ **Advertising:** This includes TV and radio ads, billboards (giant signs on the sides of roads and highways), online ads, and even ads in your school's newsletter.

↳ **Promotion:** Offering discounts, coupons, or buy one, get-one-free offers to attract people to try your product or service.

↳ **Social Media:** Using platforms like Instagram, Snapchat, or TikTok to share information about your business and engage with your customers.

↳ **Word of Mouth:** This is when people talk about your product or service with their friends, family, and coworkers. It's one of the most powerful forms of marketing!

↳ **Events and Sponsorships:** Hosting a fun event or sponsoring a local team or club can help get your business's name out there in a big way.

The goal of marketing is to attract attention, create interest, and inspire people to want to learn more about (and hopefully buy!) your product or service.

MAKING MONEY WITH SOCIAL MEDIA: HOW TO BUILD YOUR ONLINE PRESENCE (AND WHAT NOT TO DO)

Alright, you've got your fabulous product or service, and you're ready to share it online with the world. But how do you get the word out?

You've probably seen your favorite celebrities or influencers on social media platforms posting fun photos, entertaining videos, and promoting products. Did you ever think about doing the same thing for your own business? Well, you can!

Social media platforms allow you to reach out to customers, both old and new, from all corners of the globe. It's a way to show people what you're all about - your products, your values, your story. You can use social media to connect with your audience, build your brand, and even sell directly to customers.

Here are some tips:

↳ **Age Restrictions:** Most platforms have age restrictions, usually requiring users to be at least 13 years old. If you aren't old enough, there are many other ways to market so don't break the rules. Before using any platform, consult with your parents.

↳ **Be extremely careful with personal information:** Always remember that the internet is a public place. Do not **EVER** share personal information like your home address, phone number, financial information, or private details about your life. Safety first!

↳ **Choose the right platform:** Think about where your potential customers are likely to hang out online. If your product is something that needs to be seen, like clothing or art, Instagram might be a good fit. If you're great at explaining things and want to share information, try making videos for YouTube.

↳ **Be consistent**: You must post regularly and create content that is interesting. You don't have to post every day but create a schedule and stick to it.

↳ **Be authentic:** Be genuine and honest about your products, services, and business practices. Building trust with your audience is important for long-term success. Let your true personality shine!

↳ **Engage with your followers:** Reply to comments, ask questions in your

posts, and show appreciation for your customers. This helps to build a community around your brand.

→ **Use hashtags wisely:** Hashtags can help people find your content. Research popular hashtags in your industry or create a unique one for your brand.

→ **Don't buy followers:** It might be tempting to pay for a boost in followers, but don't do it. It's better to have a smaller number of genuine followers who are interested in your business than to have a bunch of fake followers.

→ **Pay attention to your digital footprint**: Everything you post leaves a permanent digital footprint. Be careful about what you share and make sure it's positive and professional.

→ **Get Permission and Respect Privacy:** Before you post about customers or anyone else, be sure to get permission from them. Respecting privacy shows respect for others and helps build trust with your audience.

→ **Handle feedback and criticism gracefully:** Social media platforms provide a space for people to express their opinions, both positive and negative. Use all feedback as an opportunity to learn, grow, and improve your business. Feel free to address concerns and provide good customer service, but there's no need to respond or defend yourself if feedback is harsh. In fact, if you get feedback or comments that hurt your feelings, immediately share it with a trusted adult so that you can come up with a strategy that makes sense for you and your business.

Remember, social media is a powerful tool that can help build your business. But you need to check with your parents before making any decisions about using it. They can provide guidance, help you understand platform guidelines, and make sure your online activities align with their expectations and your personal safety.

BEYOND SOCIAL MEDIA: OTHER GREAT WAYS TO LET PEOPLE KNOW WHAT YOU'RE SELLING

There are plenty of great ways to let people know about your business beyond social media and it's important try out different techniques. Here are some options:

→ **Traditional Advertising:** Even in our digital age, old-school methods of advertising, like flyers, brochures, or newspaper ads, can still work wonders, especially if you're targeting a local audience. For example, if you've set up a lemonade stand, a bright, attractive poster at the local community center might draw more customers than a social media post.

→ **Word of Mouth:** Never under-estimate the power of good old-fashioned gossip. If people love your product or service, they'll tell their friends, who'll tell their friends, and so on. You can encourage this by providing excellent customer service, asking for referrals, or even setting up a referral program that gives customers a discount or perk for bringing in new customers.

→ **Networking:** This is about making connections and building rela-tionships with other people in your community. Go to local events or join clubs and introduce your-self and your business. You never know...the person you chat with at a community picnic could be your next big customer or even a future business partner.

→ **Email Marketing:** If you have a website, a great way to keep your customers engaged is by asking them to sign up for a newsletter. You can share updates, new prod-uct announcements, or special offers. Just remember to get their permission before contacting them (it's the law) and provide valuable content so they won't want to hit 'unsubscribe'. This sort of marketing

takes a lot of work so do your research before you commit.

→ **Join Forces:** Teaming up with another entrepreneur can be a great way to get your product or service in front of a whole new audience. Look for businesses that go well with your product or service - if you're making handmade soap, for example, you could team up with a local bed and breakfast to provide their guests with toiletries.

→ **Local Fairs and Markets**: If you have a product to sell, setting up a booth at a local fair or market can be a great way to get your product in front of lots of potential new cus-tomers. Plus, you'll have the oppor-tunity to get feedback and see what other entrepreneurs are up to.

BUILDING A SIMPLE WEBSITE

Having a website is like having your own little corner on the internet. Since you control it entirely, you can share your story, your products, or services, and have a place where your custom-ers can reach you. Plus, having a web-site makes your business look even more professional. So, let's start build-ing your website.

→ **Decide Your Website's Purpose:** Before you start building, you need to have a clear understanding of what you want your website to do. Do you want to sell products? Or maybe you're creative and you want it to be a place to show off what you've made.

↳ **Choose a Website Building Plat-form:** There are many user-friendly website builders that don't require you to know any coding. They offer drag-and-drop features that make it easy to design a professional-looking website. If you're selling products, you might want to consider a platform that specializes in selling things.

↳ **Pick a Domain Name:** Your domain name is your website's address on the internet, and it's how people will find you. Try to keep it short, easy to remember, and logical for your business. Most website builders will give you a free domain name, but it will include their name (like yourbusiness.theirbusiness.com). If you want a custom domain name without the website builder's name (like yourbusiness.com), you can purchase one from a company that sells domain names for a small annual fee.

↳ **Design Your Website:** When designing your website, keep your target audience in mind. Make sure it's easy to use, the text is easy to read, and it's simple to find any important information like how to contact you or where to buy your products. Use high-quality images and use the same colors throughout the website.

↳ **Create Important Pages**: There are key pages that most websites should have:

→ *Home -* This is where visitors land when they enter your website. It should tell visitors what your business is about and guide them to other parts of your site.

→ **About** - Here's where you tell your story and introduce yourself and your business to your visitors.

→ **Products/Services** - Clearly list and describe what you're selling. Use high quality photos if you're selling products.

→ **Contact** - Make it easy for customers to reach out with questions or orders. Include your email and social media links, if you have any.

Test and Publish - Before you publish your website, make sure to test it. Click on all the links, make sure all images load properly, and check for spelling or grammar errors. Ask an adult to test it as well; two heads are better than one.

Once you're happy with it, hit publish!

Keep Updating: Your website isn't a 'set it and forget it' thing. Keep it updated with new products, blog posts or information, news, or anything else relevant to your business.

PRO-TIP: YOU WANT PEOPLE TO STAY ON YOUR WEBSITE AND, HOPEFULLY, PURCHASE YOUR PRODUCTS OR SERVICES SO DO NOT PUT LINKS TO OTHER SITES ON YOUR SITE. YOU DON'T WANT TO SEND A POTENTIAL CUSTOMER TO ANOTHER WEBSITE!

Congratulations, you're now ready to create your own website. It may seem a bit challenging at first, but with a little bit of practice, you'll have a website that you're proud to share. So go ahead, start building your little corner of the internet.

ASIA'S
FUR FRIENDLY FASHIONS AND TOYS

Asia, a creative 11-year-old girl living in sunny Santa Monica, CA, had a talent for sewing and a passion for ecology. She noticed that many pet owners in her community were looking for eco-friendly options for their furry friends, and she saw an opportunity to turn her passion into a business designing and selling eco-friendly pet clothes and toys.

With the support of her parents, Asia transformed her garage into a small workshop where she could create her unique products. As the garage filled up with clothes and toys, she soon

realized that having a workshop was not enough to make her business successful. She needed to find ways to market and sell her creations.

Asia sat down with her seventeen-year-old sister Zina and came up with a list of creative marketing strategies to promote her sustainable pet products:

Eye-Catching Flyers: Asia designed colorful and informative flyers that displayed her eco-friendly pet clothes and toys. She included details like the materials used, the benefits of sustainable products, and her contact information. She left flyers at local pet stores, veterinary clinics, at school and at the local community center. She even gave her parents flyers to share with their co-workers.

Online Presence: Asia and Zina created a website and social media accounts for the business. Asia posted pictures of her adorable pet clothes and toys, shared stories of happy pets wearing her creations, and educated her online followers about the importance of sustainability in pet products. She encouraged her customers to share pictures of their pets enjoying her products, creating an engaged community of pet lovers.

Working with Local Pet Businesses: Asia reached out to local pet stores and groomers to form partnerships. She offered her sustainable products for sale in their stores and provided them with flyers to promote her business. In return, they recommended her products to their customers, creating a win-win situation for everyone involved.

Participating in Pet Events: Asia set up a booth at local pet events and fairs. She displayed her unique pet clothes and toys, allowing pet owners to see and feel the quality of her products firsthand. She engaged with potential customers, answered their questions, and shared the story behind her sustainable brand.

Asia's marketing strategies raised awareness about her sustainable pet clothing and toys, and pet owners in her community appreciated her commitment to the environment and were eager to support her business. Her colorful flyers, online presence, and participation in pet events helped her reach a wider audience and build loyal followers and relationships with other businesses.

SUGGESTED ACTIVITY:
DESIGN A CREATIVE FLYER FoR YoUR BUSINESS

It's time to let your creativity shine and craft a beautiful flyer for your business. Flyers are a fantastic way to spread the word about your business locally. Here's a step-by-step guide to help you out:

MATERIALS YOU'LL NEED:
- Paper (colored or white)
- Colored pens or pencils/markers
- Glitter, stickers, or any other decorations you'd like (optional)
- Computer with a graphic design program (optional)

INSTRUCTIONS

1. **Brainstorm:** What do you want your flyer to look like? Do you want it colorful and bright or simple and clean? Do you want to use hand drawings or graphic art?

2. **Design:** On a piece of paper or your computer, start designing the flyer. Make sure to include your business name, what you're offering (product or service), and how people can contact you or find out more about your business.

3. **Add Some Details**: Make your flyer stand out by adding fun facts about your business, a customer review, or a special offer (like a discount or buy-one-get-one-free).

4. **Make it Eye-catching:** Use colors, different fonts, and images to make your flyer attractive and exciting. You want people to be curious and want to know more about your business.

5. **Review and Print:** Check your flyer for any errors. If you're satisfied with it, get permission, and print out as many copies as you need.

6. **Distribute:** With adult permission, pass out flyers in your neighborhood, at school (with permission), or on community bulletin boards.

The goal of this activity is to use your creativity, communication skills, and marketing knowledge to design a flyer that will get people interested in your business, so have fun with it!

HERE'S A SAMPLE FLYER OUTLINE FOR A DOG WALKING BUSINESS:

[Header: Eye-Catching Title]
Doggy Delight Dog Walking Services

[Image: Illustration of a happy dog walking with a leash]

[Subtitle: Catchy Slogan]
"Pawsome Walks for Happy Tails!"

[Main Text]
Are you too busy to give your furry friend the exercise they need? Look no further! Doggy Delight Dog Walking Services is here to help! Our team of responsible and friendly dog walkers is ready to give your pup the wag-tastic walk they deserve.

[Service Highlights]
- Fun-filled walks that fit to your dog's needs
- Professional and caring dog walkers
- Flexible scheduling
- Competitive prices that can't be beat!

[Contact Information]
Phone: [Your Phone Number]
Email: [Your Email Address]
Website: [Your Website, if applicable]

[Footer: Call-to-Action]
Book your dog's first walk today and experience the joy of a happy and healthy pup!

[Background: Paw Prints or Dog-Themed Design]

Note: Before you advertise your business or take customers, be sure that you and your parents or guardians check any local rules about advertising or running a business.

Chapter 10:

BUILDING YOUR STRENGTHS: THE ENTREPRENEURIAL TOOLKIT

If you don't like
the road you're walking,
start paving another one.

DOLLY PARTON
Singer-Songwriter
and Entrepreneur

So, WHAT ARE THE SUPER SKILLS THAT ENTREPRENEURS NEED?

⤷ **Creativity**: Entrepreneurs are idea people They constantly think of new products, services, or solutions to problems. They're not afraid to dream big and think outside of the box. Remember, Lily's healthy snack idea? That's the power of creativity.

⤷ **Resilience**: Not everything always goes according to plan. Entrepreneurs often face obstacles, from a product idea failing to a customer giving bad feedback. But successful entrepreneurs are resilient which means that they view setbacks as learning experiences and opportunities rather than failures, and they don't give up.

⤷ **Decision-Making**: Entrepreneurs make lots of decisions, from big ones like what kind of business to start, to small ones like which logo design to choose. They need to look at options, consider risks, and make decisions confidently.

⤷ **People Skills**: Entrepreneurs may work with many people, including customers, employees, suppliers, and investors. Good people skills help them build strong relationships, and work well with others.

⤷ **Financial Smarts:** Understanding money matters is essential for entrepreneurs. They need to know how to manage money, make budgets, and understand costs and profits.

⤷ **Adaptability:** The business world can change quickly. New competitors pop up, and unexpected events can happen. Successful entrepreneurs are able to adjust their plans and strategies when needed.

⤷ **Leadership:** As the heads of their businesses, entrepreneurs need to be good leaders. They are responsible for guiding their team, making important decisions, and inspiring others to work towards the goals of the business.

In the next section, we'll talk about how to develop these skills and grow from setbacks. Every skill can be learned and improved with practice!

GROWING FROM FAILURES AND SETBACKS

Now that we've learned about the essential skills every entrepreneur needs, let's talk about a secret weapon that's not really a skill, but more of a mindset: the power to grow from failures and setbacks.

Entrepreneurs often come across challenges that can seem overwhelming. An idea might not work as planned, a product might not sell, or a deal might not go through. These are hard moments, but they're also incredible opportunities for growth.

Here's how you can turn setbacks into comebacks:

↳ **Don't Fear Failure:** Failure isn't the opposite of success, it's a part of it. Every successful entrepreneur has had their share of setbacks. It's all about how you respond to these moments that counts.

↳ **Learn from Your Mistakes**: When something doesn't go as planned, don't ignore it. Become a detective! Investigate what happened and why. Was there something you could've done differently? This isn't about blaming yourself; it's about learning valuable lessons for the future. It's an opportunity to rethink your ideas and come back stronger. If something doesn't work, come up with an even better idea.

↳ **Stay Positive and Resilient:** Keep your spirits up, even when times are tough. Believe in yourself. Resilience isn't about never falling down; it's about always getting back up.

↳ **Seek Support**: Don't be afraid to ask for help. Whether it's a mentor, a family member, or a friend, other people can offer advice, share their own experiences, and provide comfort during difficult times.

The key is to see each challenge as a steppingstone, not a stumbling block. So, when you face a setback, don't let it get you down. Learn from it!

CYCLE FIXERS RISE TO THE CHALLENGE

Two twelve-year-old best friends, Kaley, and LaTanya, decided to start a business together. They called it 'Cycle Fixers,' an onsite bicycle repair and maintenance service for their fellow bike enthusiasts in Grant Park, a neighborhood in Atlanta, GA. They combined Kaley's passion for fixing bikes and LaTanya's talent for problem-solving. It seemed like a perfect match!

Everything started off great. They sharpened their bicycle repair skills by fixing not only their own bikes but those of friends and siblings and received thumbs-up from everyone. They had a plan to offer their services right in their neighborhood, making it convenient for bike owners and they were excited to get started.

Soon after the business launched, the neighborhood experienced a lot of bike malfunctions and punctured tires. Kaley and LaTanya were ready to roll up their sleeves and fix the bikes, but there was a problem—they couldn't carry all their tools and supplies around the neighborhood. It seemed like their business would come to a screeching halt before it even got off the ground.

But they didn't let the challenge deflate their spirits. They put their heads together and came up with a creative solution.

The girls decided to set up a small workshop in Kaley's parents' garage, where they could repair the bikes. They spread the word about their workshop through flyers, local community groups, and their school bulletin board, highlighting the convenience of their onsite services and quick turnaround times.

To make it even more appealing, they introduced a special deal for the first month—10% off on all repairs and free air pumping for tires. They believed that this would encourage more people to give their services a try.

Their plan worked like a charm! Bike owners in Grant Park were thrilled to have Cycle Fixers nearby. They appreciated the convenience of the onsite repairs and the expertise of the young entrepreneurs. Word spread quickly, and soon they were booked with appointments.

Kaley and LaTanya's solution not only helped them overcome challenges but also attracted new customers and built a reputation for their business. They turned a setback into an opportunity for growth and success.

Their story is an example for all young entrepreneurs. Challenges are not roadblocks; they are chances to think creatively and find solutions. Kaley and LaTanya's determination and adaptability paid off, proving that with the right mindset and a bit of innovation, anything is possible.

Chapter 11:

SECURING YOUR FINANCIAL FUTURE

It's not how good you are,
it's how good you want to be.

DR. SEUSS
The Cat in The Hat

NOW IT'S TIME TO LEARN HOW TO WISELY MANAGE THE MONEY YOU EARN. THIS IS WHERE FINANCIAL LITERACY COMES IN.

So, what is financial literacy? It's the ability to understand and use different financial skills, including personal financial management, budgeting, and investing. Being financially literate can help you make good decisions about your money, and it's an important skill for everyone, not just business owners.

Learning about money might seem complicated or even boring, but it's not at all. In fact, understanding how money works can be like unlocking a superpower, and the sooner you learn, the better. Here's why:

↳ **Making Smart Money Choices:** When you understand money, you can make smart choices about spending, saving, and investing your earnings. For example, you'll know how to create a budget, which can help you avoid overspending.

↳ **Planning for the Future:** Financial literacy helps you understand the importance of saving for things you want to buy in the future, like a new bicycle or even a car when you're older. It also helps you plan for unexpected expenses like buying a new laptop for your business when you need to.

↳ **Understanding Value:** It helps you understand the idea that some things are worth spending more on than others, and that some things are 'nice to have' but not 'necessary.'

↳ **Avoiding Scams:** Unfortunately, there are people and businesses out there who take advantage of individuals who aren't financially literate. Understanding how money works can help protect you from scams and fraud.

↳ **Building Wealth:** Being financially literate can help you build wealth. You'll know how to invest your money so that it can grow over time.

We'll explore key concepts around protecting and investing your earnings. Get ready to level up your money skills!

PROTECTING YOUR MONEY: BUDGETING AND SAVING STRATEGIES

Now that you understand why financial literacy is important, let's move on to two important money management skills: budgeting and saving. These two skills will help you protect and grow your earnings.

Budgeting: Think of a budget as a plan for your money. It helps you keep track of what you earn, spend, and save.

Creating a personal budget is simple. First, you need to figure out how much money you're earning from your business each month as well as how much you get as an allowance and any gift money you expect to receive. This is your income. Next, you need to figure out how much you're spending. This includes costs to keep your business running and any money you spend on personal things like toys, games, or outings with friends. These are your expenses.

Once you know your income and expenses, you subtract your expenses from your income. The amount left over is what you have available to save or invest.

Income - Expenses = Saving or Investing

Saving: Saving money is like building a safety net for your future. It can help you buy things you want, or help you cover unexpected costs.

There are many ways to save money, but here are a few strategies:

Set Savings Goals: Do you have something specific you want to save for? Maybe it's a new skateboard, a trip, or a new business idea. Having a specific goal can make saving more exciting and rewarding.

Save First: One great saving strategy is to save first. This means that as soon as you earn income from your business, receive your allowance or birthday money, you put a portion of it into your savings before you do anything else. This is called "paying yourself first."

Savings Account: A savings account is a type of bank account where you can store your money safely and earn a small amount of interest (extra money) over time. Here's how you might use a savings account:

→ **1. Open a savings account**: You can do this at a local bank or credit union. You'll need a parent or guardian to help set up the account if you're under 18.

→ **2. Deposit money into the account**: After your account is set up, you can start putting money into it. This can be done by depositing cash or checks at the bank, or by transferring money from another account.

→ **3. Watch your savings grow:** Your bank will pay you a small amount of interest on the money in your savings account. The more money you save, the more interest you'll earn.

↳ *Checking Account*: A checking account is another type of bank account, but it's designed for regular use. You can deposit and withdraw money frequently, and you can also use a debit card linked to the account to make purchases or withdraw money from ATMs. Again, you'll need an adult to help you set this up if you're under 18.

↳ *Online Saving:* There are many ways to save money online, and these can be particularly handy for a young entrepreneur. Here are a few:

↳ **Online Savings Accounts:** These work like a regular savings account, but they're online. They often pay higher interest and can be easier to manage because you can transfer money and check your balance anytime you want.

↳ **Money Management Apps:** There are lots of apps that can help you save money. Some round up the change from your purchases and put it into savings, while others let you set goals and track your progress.

↳ **Direct Deposit:** If you earn money from your business electronically, you may be able to set up direct deposit which is automatically transferring a part of your earnings into your savings account.

↳ **Prepaid Cards:** You load a specific amount of money onto the card for spending, which can help you stick to your budget. Just be aware that some prepaid cards have fees.

It's important to check with a parent or guardian before setting up any new accounts or using financial apps. They can help you understand the fine print and make sure you're making the best choices for your financial future.

Budgeting and saving aren't about restricting what you can do with your money, they're about helping you to make smart decisions and reach your financial goals. They are essential parts of financial literacy and important tools for securing your financial future.

Chapter 12:

LOOKING AHEAD:
THE FUTURE IS YOURS!

Do not wait for someone else
to come and speak for you.
It's you who can change the world.

MALALA YOUSAFZAI
Nobel Peace Prize laureate and Activist.

YOU'VE ALREADY TAKEN SOME EXCITING STEPS TO BECOMING AN ENTREPRENEUR. BUT THE PATH IS NOT A SHORT SPRINT; IT'S A MARATHON. THE LEARNING NEVER REALLY ENDS.

HERE ARE SOME WAYS YOU CAN CONTINUE TO GROW AS AN ENTREPRENEUR:

↳ **Always Be Curious:** Just like you, the world around us is constantly changing and evolving. New technologies, new trends, and new opportunities emerge all the time. So, keep asking questions, keep exploring, and always be open to learning new things.

↳ **Take Risks and Learn from Mistakes:** Remember, making mistakes is not a sign of failure but a part of the learning process. The most successful entrepreneurs are those who are willing to take risks, make mistakes, learn from them, and then try again.

↳ **Seek Feedback and Listen:** Other people can provide valuable perspectives that can help you grow. Whether it's customers, mentors, or fellow entrepreneurs, be open to their feedback. Listen, learn, and use their suggestions to improve.

↳ **Keep an Entrepreneur's Mindset:** An entrepreneur's mindset is all about seeing opportunities where others see obstacles. It's about being creative, taking initiative, and being persistent. Remember to keep this mindset as you continue your journey.

↳ **Never Stop Dreaming:** Even if your first business idea doesn't work out as you hoped, don't stop dreaming. Successful entrepreneurs often try many ideas before finding one that really takes off.

↳ **Stay Healthy:** Being an entrepreneur can be stressful, and it's easy to forget to take care of yourself. Your health is important so be sure to eat healthily, exercise, get enough sleep, and take breaks when you need them. Any time you feel yourself getting overwhelmed or stressed out, take a break and do something fun that you love. As an entrepreneur, student, and family member, it's important to find balance in the things that you do and enjoy yourself!

BEYOND ENTREPRENEURSHIP: DEVELOPING AS A LEADER

You might be wondering, "Isn't being an entrepreneur already being a leader?" While it's true that entrepreneurs are leaders within their businesses, leadership goes beyond entrepreneurship. As a leader, you have the power to inspire others, to make a difference in your community, and to change the world. Here's how you can continue to develop as a leader:

→ **Build Empathy:** Great leaders can understand and share the feelings of others. This is known as empathy. By understanding the people around you, you'll be better able to inspire and motivate them.

→ **Encourage Teamwork:** Leaders know that they can't do everything on their own. They need a team, and they know how to encourage their team to work together. Teamwork skills can be learned and strengthened through group projects, sports, and other collaborative activities.

→ **Learn to Communicate Effectively**: Leaders are great communicators. They can express their ideas and they are also excellent listeners. You can improve your communication skills by reading as much as possible, participating in debates or public speaking activities, and paying close attention and asking questions during conversations, which is a skill called active listening.

→ **Practice Decision-Making:** Leaders must make tough decisions. You can develop this skill by taking on leadership roles in clubs, sports, or group projects. Practice analyzing situations, considering options, and making decisions.

→ **Be a Role Model:** Good leaders lead by example. Whether it's through hard work, empathy, or being honest and having strong moral principles (*integrity*), try to be someone others can look up to.

Leadership is not about having power over others; it's about helping others to be stronger. Think about how you can use your abilities to lead and inspire those around you. Who knows, maybe one day, you'll be the one inspiring the next generation of young entrepreneurs!

PAIGE'S
BOOK SWAP

When Paige was 10, she started out with a simple idea. She loved books but noticed that many of her classmates did not share her enthusiasm. They struggled to find books that they found interesting. Paige saw this as a challenge. With her parents' help, she created a book swap platform for kids, which she operated from her garage at the beginning. The platform allowed children to swap books they had finished reading for others they hadn't read yet.

As Paige entered middle school, she realized that her book swap idea could help not only her classmates but also children who couldn't afford books. She started fundraising to add new books to her platform and opened her swap to schools in lower-income neighborhoods.

Paige's initiative caught the attention of a local newspaper, and she was given an opportunity to talk about her project on a local radio station. This exposure attracted the interest of a local used bookstore, which offered to partner with Paige by giving customers a discounted rate for books bought through her platform.

Fast forward five years, Paige is now a leader in her field. She didn't stop at the book swap platform. She used the skills and knowledge she gained to start other projects, including an app that recommends personalized book suggestions for kids, and a virtual book club. She even organized a citywide book festival for children and teens.

Paige's story shows that entrepreneurship is not just about making money. It's about seeing a problem or a need, coming up with a solution, and taking the initiative to make that solution a reality. But Paige's story also shows how entrepreneurship can be a springboard for leadership. She has become a role model for other young entrepreneurs, demonstrating that age is no barrier to success in business or leadership.

Paige's journey from young entrepreneur to industry leader didn't happen overnight. It took time, effort, learning, and growth. And like Paige, as you continue your entrepreneurial journey, remember that the skills and experiences you gain can lead you to great places not only in business but also in life. The future is truly in your hands!

SUGGESTED ACTIVITY: REFLECTING ON YOUR ENTREPRENEURIAL JOURNEY AND SETTING FUTURE GOALS

INSTRUCTIONS

1. **Think About Your Journey**: Look back at everything you've learned in this book. What were some of the most important lessons for you? Write a brief paragraph describing where you are on your entrepreneurial journey, the challenges you may have faced, how you overcame them, and the successes you've had. If you haven't started a business of your own yet, that's ok. You can reflect on what you think might happen when you do get started.

2. **Imagine Your Future**: Imagine you are five years into the future. Where do you see yourself? Are you running your own business, leading a team, or maybe even starting a new project? Draw a picture or create a collage that represents your vision of the future. You could include things like a logo for your future business, pictures of people who inspire you, or symbols that represent your goals.

3. **Set Your Goals:** Set at least three goals for yourself. These could be short-term goals (like learning a new skill or improving your product) or long-term goals (like expanding your business or starting a new project). Make sure your goals are SMART: *Specific, Measurable, Achievable, Relevant,* and *Time-bound.* For example, instead of saying "I want to sell more products," a SMART goal would be "I want to sell 100 lightbulbs in the next three months."

4. **Develop an Action Plan:** For each goal, write down at least three steps you need to take to achieve it. These should be specific actions that will move you closer to your goal.

5. **Share Your Goals:** It's important to share your goals and action plan with a trusted friend, family member, or mentor. They can provide feedback, offer support, and help you stay on track as you work toward your goals.

With clear goals, a plan of action, and a willingness to continue learning and growing, there's no limit to what you can achieve!

Chapter 13:

PARENTS' GUIDE To NURTURING ENTREPRENEURIAL MINDS

You have to believe in yourself
when no one else does.
That's what makes you a winner.

VENUS WILLIAMS
Professional Tennis Player,
and Entrepreneur

AS A PARENT, SEEING YOUR CHILD EXPRESS INTEREST IN ENTREPRENEURSHIP CAN BE BOTH EXCITING AND A BIT OVERWHELMING. THE PATH CAN BE FILLED WITH CREATIVE THINKING, PROBLEM-SOLVING, RISK-TAKING, AND LEARNING FROM FAILURES.

The entrepreneurial journey often begins with a simple idea, an observation, or a problem your child wants to solve. They may talk about wanting to start a business or make a product. They might come up with wild, imaginative ideas that may not always seem practical. The key here is to give them room to explore. That can be tough when you don't necessarily have entrepreneurial experience yourself.

But just as you do in other aspects of your role as a parent, all you really need to do is to listen, support, and guide (and try to avoid directing). Your child will need to learn to make decisions, take risks, and bounce back from failures. This process can teach them responsibility and self-confidence, as well as practical skills like planning, budgeting, and thinking about their financial futures.

While it may be tempting to step in and try to "fix" things when they encounter difficulties, it's essential to let them experience the difficulties. These experiences will help them build resilience and learn critical problem-solving skills.

Every child's entrepreneurial experience will be unique. What works for one may not work for another. Your child might take a different path than the one you envision for them, but that's okay. It's all about creating a love of learning and figuring out how to do hard things. Here are ways you can create a supportive environment for your child:

↳ **Encourage Curiosity:** Ask open-ended questions that stimulate thought and provoke curiosity. Promote discussions about different topics and listen to their ideas without judgment. This will foster a love for learning and spark innovative thinking.

↳ **Value Creativity:** Provide them with resources and materials that encourage creative exploration. This could include anything from art supplies to science kits or tools for coding. Allow them to dream big and support their creative ventures.

↳ **Promote Resilience:** You can teach your child that failure is a stepping-stone to success. Let them know that it's okay to make mistakes and encourage them to try again when they fail. This will help them develop the resilience needed for not only entrepreneurship, but for life.

↳ **Create a Balanced Schedule and Prioritize Time Management**: Kids can get excited about new projects, prioritizing their new business venture at the expense of education or other activities. Creating a balanced schedule that includes time for school, entrepreneurship, physical activities, and fun and relaxation can be a family project that everyone gets involved in.

You can teach your child the importance of managing their time effectively by introducing them to tools and techniques such as planners, calendars, or digital apps that can help them organize their tasks. Creating a consistent daily and weekly schedule can help them stay on track. Be flexible - the schedule can change as required, but having a structure provides a good starting point.

↳ **Build Financial Literacy:** When you teach your kids basic financial concepts such as budgeting, saving, and investing, that knowledge will serve them well in life. It is genuinely never too early to get started applying the principles in practical ways. Even preschoolers can be introduced to the concept of saving by using a piggy bank. If we teach our kids how to manage money before they go off into the world, we set them up to avoid pitfalls that can be big but entirely preventable.

As parents we can sometimes treat money as if it's a taboo topic or too complex to discuss with our kids. But if we treat money like the everyday, and necessary, thing that it is, we can position them to make informed and sound decisions when we're not around. I got my first credit card when I was in grad school. I had no income, but I used that card like it was cash. I don't have to tell you that the consequences were...not great. I promised myself that I would teach my kids how to manage money and avoid unnecessary outcomes.

↳ **Provide Real-World Exposure:** You can provide opportunities for your child to experience the real business world. This could be through visits to local businesses, participating in youth entrepreneurship programs, or attending business-focused events and workshops.

When you provide an environment where your kids can explore, learn, and grow on their own, you nurture their passions and guide them towards realizing their own dreams and aspirations.

↳ **Teach the Importance of Rest:** It's important for children to understand that rest and relaxation are not just rewards for hard work, but essential parts of maintaining

Startup Smart: The Girls' Guide to Entrepreneurship

mental and physical health. Making sure your child is getting enough sleep and taking breaks when they need to can help them learn to take care of themselves.

→ **Promote the Value of Education and Effective Study Skills:** While your child may be excited about their business, it's crucial they understand the value of their education. Help them see how what they're learning in school can benefit their business, from math skills aiding in understanding finances and profits, to language skills assisting in marketing and communication.

Effective study skills can reduce the time it takes to complete schoolwork while improving the quality of work. Teaching your child how to break big assignments into smaller, manageable tasks, and to tackle the most challenging tasks when they are most alert can create habits that will serve them well throughout life.

→ **Foster Problem-Solving:** Balancing various commitments will naturally lead to some conflicts and challenges. Use these as opportunities to develop your child's problem-solving abilities. It can be tempting to jump in and solve things for them. While it may be faster and more efficient, it doesn't

allow them to grow and learn to troubleshoot.

SAFEGUARDING YoUR CHILD'S INTERESTS

As important as it is to encourage your child's entrepreneurial enthusiasm, it's equally crucial to ensure their well-being and protect their interests. Here are things you've likely considered, but it can't hurt to reiterate:

→ **Overseeing Online Activities:** If your child's business idea involves the internet, be sure to monitor their online activities to ensure they are safe. This includes who they interact with, the information they share, and the websites they visit.

→ **Privacy and Personal Information:** Teach your child the importance of not sharing personal information without your approval. This applies to online and offline interactions. They should understand the potential risks and implications of sharing personal details.

→ **Understanding Contracts and Agreements:** If there are any contracts or agreements to sign in relation to your child's business, be sure to review these carefully before giving your consent. It's always advisable to consult with a legal professional in such cases.

- **Guidance with Business Decisions:** Even though your child is the one running the business, they might need your guidance when it comes to making significant business decisions. Use these opportunities to teach them about ethical business practices and responsible decision-making.

- **Respecting School Commitments:** As exciting as a new business can be, school remains the priority, so it can help to remind them of the importance of continuing to do their best. No matter how well their business venture does, they will always benefit from their formal education.

As the guiding force in your child's life, your attitude toward entrepreneurship can profoundly influence their outlook. Have fun with it!

For additional resources for young entrepreneurs and their families visit:
http://TheBoldestMeKids.com

www.ingramcontent.com/pod-product-compliance
Lightning Source LLC
Chambersburg PA
CBHW081153090426
42736CB00017B/3308